Raniero Cantalamessa, O.F.M. Cap.

The Mystery of Easter

Alan Neame, Translator

A Liturgical Press Book

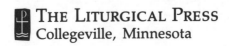

THE LITURGICAL PRESS
Collegeville, Minnesota

Cover design by Ann Blattner.
Icon: The Descent into Hell, School of Dionysius (15th century), Russian Museum, St. Petersburg.

Published originally in Italian under the title *Il Mistero Pasquale* by Editrice Ancora Milano.

4   5   6   7   8   9

Library of Congress Cataloging-in-Publication Data

Cantalamessa, Raniero.
    [Mistero Pasquale. English]
    The mystery of Easter / Raniero Cantalamessa ; Alan Neame, translator.
       p.   cm.
    ISBN 0-8146-2129-5
    1. Easter.   2. Paschal mystery.   3. Catholic Church—Liturgy.
    4. Spiritual life-Catholic Church.   I. Title.
    BV55.C3313   1993
    232'.5—dc 20   93-24303
                                                    CIP

Contents

Chapter One

"What Does This Rite Mean?"

The Paschal Mystery in the Bible and the Fathers

Scarcely had the feast of Passover come into being in Israel than the question arose as to what exactly it meant: "What does this rite of yours mean?" (Exod 12:26). Always asked at the beginning of the Jewish Passover supper, the question was to accompany the story of the feast down the ages, inviting all who heard it to a progressively deeper understanding of its meaning. The question is the same in function as that other one, found too in Christian sources: "What do we commemorate tonight?" or again: "Why do we keep vigil on this night?"[1] It is important since it serves to identify the salvific event that lies at the origin of the Passover: in other words, what precisely the Passover is a "memorial" of. So too for us Christians this question can be a valuable tool for acquiring an ever deeper understanding of the paschal mystery and, more important still, for adopting as our own that understanding which others before us have had of it.

1. The two faces of the Passover

To the question: "What does this rite mean?", the Old Testament gives two different but complementary answers. According to the more ancient explanation, the feast of Passover primarily commemorates "the Passover of God." This word *Passover* was supposedly derived from a verb indicating the action of God, who "passes over," in the sense of skipping, or sparing, or protecting the homes of the Hebrews while striking those of their foes: "When your children ask you, 'What does this rite of yours mean?', you shall reply, 'This is the Passover sacrifice [*pesach*] of the LORD, who passed over [*pasachti*] the houses of the Israelites in Egypt; when he struck down the Egyptians, he spared our houses'" (Exod 12:26-27).

7

The content, or the event, which the Passover commemorates is therefore the saving passage of God: Passover because God passed over! This is an explanation of the Passover which may be defined as *theological* or *theocentric* since in it the protagonist is God. The emphasis is entirely on the divine initiative, that is to say on the cause, rather than on the effect, of being saved.

In Deuteronomy and in other less ancient parts of the Book of Exodus itself, attention shifts from the moment of sacrificing the lamb to that of the Exodus from Egypt, which is seen as a passing from slavery to freedom (cf. Deut 16 and Exod 13–15). With the changing of the central event, the protagonist or subject of the Passover changes too: no longer is it God who passes and saves, but human beings, the people, who pass and are saved. This is an interpretation of the Passover which may be defined as *anthropological* or *anthropocentric.* I have already said that we are dealing with two complementary, not mutually exclusive, answers. Human beings, even in this second explanation, are seen as dependent on God; the Exodus prepares for the Sinaitic Covenant! So here we have a religious liberation, not a political one (at least, not primarily a political one). The nation is set free to serve God, as the biblical sources so often say: "Let my people go, so that they may serve me" (cf. Exod 4:23; 5:1).

This twofold interpretation—theological and anthropological—continues throughout the entire Old Testament. At the time of Jesus we find this inconsistent situation. In *official Palestinian Judaism*, dominated by the Temple and the Jewish priesthood, the theological interpretation holds sway: the Passover primarily commemorates the passing of God. There is a very fine text in which salvation history is summed up in four fundamental events: the creation of the world, the sacrifice of Isaac, the Passover, and the end of the world (the "four nights"). In this particular text, the Passover is described as "the night in which God manifested himself against the Egyptians and protected the firstborn of Israel"[2] In this environment—which was the environment of Jesus—the Passover presents a strongly ritual and sacrificial aspect. It consists, that is to say, in a concrete liturgy, the essential moments of which are the sacrificing of the lamb in the Temple at dusk on the 14 Nisan, and the eating of it in family groups the same night at the Passover supper.

In *Hellenistic or Diaspora Judaism*, on the other hand, the anthropological explanation predominates: there the central histor-

8

ical event commemorated by the Passover is the people's crossing of the Red Sea. But even this is relegated to second place, as regards the allegorical meaning of the event which is "the passing of the individual from slavery to freedom, from vice to virtue." The most famous representative of this school of thought writes: "The feast of Passover is a memorial of and a thanksgiving for the great emigration from Egypt. But for those who are accustomed to turning what they are told into allegory, the feast of Passover signifies the purification of the soul." "Properly speaking, Passover means the passing over from all passion to that which is intelligible and divine."[3] Migration, exodus, passing over, exit are images of great spiritual resonance, especially if seen in the context of that biblical mentality which regarded Abram's emigration, and indeed emigration in general, as the physical model of the faith and destiny of Israel ("My father was a *wandering* Aramaean . . .") and which was to be extended in the New Testament in the ideal of living as "aliens and sojourners" (1 Pet 2:11; Heb 11:13).

If the Passover is essentially the passing over from vice to virtue, evidently it will not have God for subject, but human beings, and it will not be celebrated so much with a liturgy and outward ceremonies (though these will not be repudiated) as with a continual and inner striving towards the good. The paschal lamb to be offered to God is one's own spiritual progress, Philo said, going back to the etymological meaning of the Greek term used to designate the paschal victim (*probaton,* lamb, kid-goat, coming from *probaino,* meaning I go forward, I progress).

Thus we have seen two mutually contrasting paschal concepts take shape; these will survive into Christianity and, with their dialectic, mold all paschal spirituality right to our own day.

Let us pass on then from the Jewish to the Christian Passover. But, first of all, one question: when did a Christian feast of Passover first come into existence? The primitive Christian community, after the death of Jesus, though it continued for a little while to "go up to the Temple" and celebrate the Passover with the rest of the Jews, began at a certain point to regard and live this annual festival no longer as a memorial of the events of the Exodus and as a waiting for the *coming* of the Messiah, but rather as a memorial of what a few years earlier had happened in Jerusalem at one particular Passover and as a waiting for the *return* of Christ. The inward dissociation preceded the ritual one and the

Christian feast of the Passover was celebrated "in spirit and in truth" in the depth of the disciples' hearts before it acquired a rite and feast day of its own. This, however, was not long in coming, once the inward transformation of the Passover's content had taken place within them. And perhaps, when St. Paul in 1 Corinthians 5:8 exhorts his converts "to celebrate the feast," it is already to the Christian feast that he is alluding. Thus it came about that the yearly return of the Passover came to be celebrated by the disciples with a special feast day, the novelty of which they became increasingly aware.

How did such a swift and sharply defined transplantation of the paschal institution from Old to New Testament, from Israel to the Church, take place? Apparently the point of contact was a purely *chronological* fact: Christ died (and rose again) in Jerusalem, on the occasion of a Jewish Passover. For St. John the Evangelist, his death actually coincided with the sacrificing of the paschal lambs in the Temple. This chronological datum alone would certainly not have been enough to work the grand transformation of the Passover, if within it another, stronger datum had not been at work: the *typological* one. That event—the sacrificing of Christ—was seen as fulfilling all the figures and all the expectations in the old Passover. Melito of Sardis expresses this conviction in words that deliberately follow very closely the Johannine treatment of the incarnation, as though inferring that the Easter mystery is but the last line and consistent conclusion of a process that began with the incarnation:

> The law has become Word,
> the old has become the new,
> the figure has become reality
> and the lamb become the Son.[4]

In the light of this event, the New Testament writers were to reinterpret the entire Jesus-story, seeing in it the definitive fulfillment of the old Passover.

The Church has thus inherited her Passover feast from Israel; but in its passage from Israel to the Church it has changed its content; it has become the memorial of something else. And so once more we ask the ancient question: "What does this rite mean?"

10

2. The Passover as Passion

At the heart of Christianity too, two complementary answers emerge, constituting the two main paschal traditions of the primitive Church. To start with, until the third century, from the point of view of theological content (not of liturgical practice!) there is basically a unitary paschal tradition. This is the tradition which by reason of its place of origin and greatest flowering, Asia Minor, is known as "Asiatic." We are talking about a *Christological* or *Christocentric Passover of historico-commemorative and eschatological content,* that is to say, a Passover having as protagonist, not human beings, nor the God of the Old Testament, but Jesus Christ. Of Christ it commemorates—and this is why it is called "commemorative"—all "the new and old mystery: new in the reality, old in the prefiguration of it" (Melito). In other words, Easter commemorates all salvation history, culminating in Jesus Christ and stretching forward in expectation of his second coming—which is why it is also said to be "eschatological." In a similar context, we find the bold affirmation: "The Passover is Christ!" (Justin and Melito).

Where Christ is concerned, however, the Passover above all commemorates "his great sacrifice" (Apolinarius of Hierapolis), his passion, so much so that the very word *Pascha* is thought to come from the Greek verb meaning "to suffer." "What is the Passover?" Melito asks himself and answers: "The name is derived from the event: for to celebrate the Passover [*paschein*] comes from 'having suffered' [*pathein*]."[5] For a very long time this artless etymological explanation (artless since it derives a Hebrew word from a Greek one!) was to influence the paschal theology of most Christian authors.

Theologically unitary, the paschal concept just described, for reasons and at a date none too clear, took the ritual form of two differing liturgical observances, and these gave rise to that "no small controversy" which vexed the Church in the second century in the days of Pope Victor and brought her to the brink of the first great schism. The Churches of Asia Minor, adhering more closely to the Jewish Passover and the authority of St. John (who had pointed to the sacrifice of Jesus on the cross as the paschal event *par excellence*), celebrated the Passover on 14 Nisan, whichever day of the week it might fall on (whence the name Quartodecimans was bestowed on them). The rest of Christendom,

11

however, with Rome at its head, celebrated it on the Sunday following 14 Nisan, that is to say, on a fixed day of the week, rather than on a fixed day of the month. Naturally, the fact of choosing the anniversary of the death or, alternatively, that of the resurrection as the date for the feast also carried with it a different accentuation of the events. In any case, the sources clearly show that, even where the feast was celebrated on the Sunday during this period, the Passover, in itself and primarily, commemorated Christ's passion. In Tertullian, for instance, the term *Pascha* always means Good Friday or the period of time from Good Friday to the night of Holy Saturday. With the vigil between the Saturday and the Sunday, the *Pascha* comes to an end and the *laetissimum spatium* of Pentecost begins. Such a preference for commemorating the passion is not surprising if we reflect that during this period of persecution the Church was herself living through a passion of her own and hence felt this moment in her Master's life to be particularly close to her own historical experience. We have this moving account by a bishop of a Passover celebrated during the storm of the Decian persecution: "They drove us out, and then alone we kept our (Passover) festival, persecuted and put to death by all. And every place where we *suffered* became a place of festive assembly for us: field, desert, ship, inn, prison. But the brightest of all Passover festivals was kept by the perfect martyrs when they feasted in heaven."[6]

The commemoration of the passion was thus far from absent among those who celebrated the Passover on the Sunday. By the same token, those who celebrated the feast on 14 Nisan, on the anniversary of Jesus' passion, did not, because of this, neglect the resurrection. For they saw Jesus' death very much through John's eyes, that is to say as "glorification," as a glorious death containing and already anticipating the resurrection. In this age of martyrdom, the very word *passio* is inseparably associated with the idea of victory and glory and, hence, of resurrection. The martyr is admitted to the celestial banquet, as St. Dionysius said above: he endures his Good Friday here below and celebrates his Resurrection Sunday in heaven.

Christ's death is at the center of the Passover in this earliest period: not the death in itself as brute fact but rather as "the death of death," as "the swallowing up of death in victory" (cf. 1 Cor 15:54). Christ's death is seen in its irrepressible vitality and saving force, by which, as St. Ignatius of Antioch says, "his passion was our resurrection."[7] And this because Jesus, as well as being human was God too and, "thanks to his Spirit which could not die, put Death to death, who slew the human race."[8]

Depending therefore on whether it was observed on Good Friday (as the Quartodecimans did) or on the Sunday (as everyone else did), the paschal mystery did indeed change in spiritual perspective and climate, but not in theological content.

3. *The Passover as Passage*

On the theological plane, the second great paschal tradition came into being in Alexandria at the beginning of the third century with Clement and Origen, who took over and Christianized that moral and spiritual concept, having humanity as central, as subject and protagonist of the Passover, which had blossomed in Hellenistic Judaism. In this new picture, the entire life of both the individual Christian and the Church is seen as an exodus, a continual journey, beginning with acceptance of the faith and ending with our leaving this world. The real Passover lies ahead, not behind; it is the celestial Passover, to be celebrated without symbols or figures in the blessed home.[9]

Now, if the Passover is primarily the passage of humanity, the stress clearly will not fall on the past so much as on the present of the Church, where alone that passage can take place. The saving events are certainly not repudiated; their importance, however, diminishes insofar as all historical events, including those concerning Christ, have a symbolic significance. Even Christ's Passover, as regards the celestial Passover, is, as St. Gregory Nazianzen says, "a figure, even if a much clearer one than that of the Law."[10] A sign that the feast has become dehistoricized is the insistence on the idea of a "continual Passover," at the expense of the anniversary Passover which is much more explicitly concerned with the historical event being commemorated.

In this tradition, the guiding principle is that "historical facts cannot be figures of other historical facts, nor can material facts be figures of other material facts, but rather of spiritual ones"[11] In other words, the historical facts of the Exodus and those relating to the death and resurrection of Jesus do not, in time present, find their main actualization in liturgical rites or outward feasts, but rather in inward and spiritual decisions and facts: thus, for example, eating the flesh of the lamb means nourishing one-self spiritually on Christ and his word.

4. *The Augustinian synthesis:*
the Passover as passage through the Passion

Such were the two main paschal traditions flourishing in the early days of the Church. To the question, What does this rite mean?, the first replied: *The passion of Christ!;* the second replied: *The passage of humanity!* We are witnessing the prolongation of the two concepts already present in the Old Testament: a theological Passover (more accurately henceforth, Christological), based on the idea of sacrifice, and an anthropological Passover, based on the idea of passage. The two views express the two protagonists and the two poles of salvation: God's initiative and the human response, grace and freedom. For some, the Passover is primarily a gift of God; for the others, it is primarily (not exclusively!) a conquest by humanity.

Subsequent writers up to the fourth century did no more than repeat, with developments, one or other of the two explanations, or join them in hybrid fashion, that is to say, without arriving at a true theological synthesis which would reduce the two views to a basic unity.

This was to be the achievement of St. Augustine. The opportunity for a revision of paschal theology arose in the Latin Church towards the end of the fourth century, when the various paschal traditions which had been developing independently of one another within the Church finally made contact, thus provoking a salutary crisis. Unlike the paschal controversy of the second century which was about the date and not the meaning of the Passover, this controversy contrariwise concerned the meaning and not the date or other liturgical elements. It remained confined, however, to theological circles and left no great mark on Church history, even though theologically speaking it was more important than the previous one.

This is what happened. Having borrowed their original paschal theology from Asia Minor, the Latins had gone on explaining the Passover as "passion." Their Passover was of the type which I have described as Christological and historico-commemorative, since it was entirely centered on Jesus Christ. A representative of this current wrote: "It is written: It is the Passover of the LORD (Exod 12:11); it is not written: of the people; for the word Passover is derived from passion; so it is called 'Passover of the LORD' because it was not the people but the Lord who at the Passover was figuratively sacrificed in the lamb."[12]

This ancient explanation of the Passover was very deeply rooted in people and clergy and was never to be entirely supplanted. (A trace of it is still to be found in the Preface for Easter Day in the Latin and Ambrosian liturgies, where the Passover is defined as "the day when Christ was immolated.") It was, however, thrown into crisis by the appearance of a new interpretation which explained the Passover as a passage. The first person to introduce it was Ambrose who, knowing Greek, was in a position, for the first time, to bring the ideas of Philo and Origen to the West, their teaching being that the Passover meant precisely the passing of human beings from vice to virtue, from sin to grace.[13]

As if this were not enough, to this first innovation was added that of Jerome who, translating the Bible from the original texts, discovered and revealed to the Latins that Passover meant, yes, passing over, but God's passing over, not humanity's: "Passover, which in Hebrew is pronounced *phase*, does not derive its name from passion, as most people maintain, but from passing . . . in the sense that the Lord 'passed over,' in coming to the help of his people."[14]

This "paschal reform" provoked a lively reaction. One of its many self-appointed spokesmen was the Ambrosiaster, who lived in Rome in the days of Pope Damasus. "Passover," he wrote, "means sacrifice and not passing, as some people are now saying; for first comes the figure of the Savior and then the sign of salvation":[15] as much as to say that the Passover should primarily commemorate the cause of salvation, which is Christ's sacrifice, and not its effect, which is humanity's passing-over.

One basic difficulty prevented these authors from reaching agreement over the Passover's significance: it lay, as yet unnoticed, in the divergence between the name and the content of the Passover. Those who interpreted the Passover as *passing-over* explained the Passover's name and its continuity with the Passover of the Old Testament but did not make equal allowance for the mysterious content and originality of the Christian Passover. In contrast, those who explained the Passover as *passion* admitted the new content of the Christian Passover (the passion and resurrection of Christ) but did not succeed in justifying the name of Passover and its relationship with the ancient institution. Why call Christ's passion "Passover," if Passover means passing-over?

Such was the dead end paschal theology had reached when, in the fullness of his maturity, Augustine too tackled the problem of the Christian Passover. He it was who resolved the seemingly insoluble conflict between the two explanations. He did this, thanks to a more careful reading of a text in John. But let us hear it in his own words: "Touching this word *Pascha,* then, which in Latin is *transitus,* i.e., 'passing-over', the blessed Evangelist, as if interpreting it to us, says, *Before the feast of Pascha, Jesus, knowing that the hour had come for him to pass from this world to the Father* . . . Lo, here is the passing-over. Whence and whither? From this world, to the Father."[16]

On the basis of this text a balance and synthesis between passion and passage, between God's Passover and humanity's Passover, between Christ's passion and resurrection, between liturgical and sacramental Passover and moral and ascetic Passover, is finally reached. Augustine took his stand on a fact which hitherto had eluded those writers who had concerned themselves with the Passover, namely, that the New Testament itself contains an explanation for the Passover's name. John, in collocating the two relevant terms *Pascha* and *to pass* (*metabaino*), intended to give a Christian interpretation and content to the word Passover. Not a few exegetes, even today, are inclined to think Augustine had hit the mark. Be that as it may, the fact is that, after Augustine, all through the Middle Ages, this was to be the favored definition of the Christian Passover: the passing of Jesus from this world to the Father.

But let us see in what way the above-listed syntheses operate, according to this definition. The passing of Jesus from this world to the Father embraces passion and resurrection very tightly; it is through his passion that Jesus attains to the glory of the resurrection. This is the quintessence of Johannine theology (cf., for instance, John 12:20-36) and of the whole New Testament. "By his passion," Augustine writes, "the Lord *passed* from death to life."[17] Passion and passing are no longer two opposing explanations but are now conjoined. The Christian Passover is a *transitus per passionem:* a passing-over through the passion. Christ's words to the disciples on the road to Emmaus at once come to mind: "Was it not necessary that the Messiah should suffer these

16

things and enter into his glory?" (Luke 24:26), and St. Paul's words: "It is necessary for us to undergo many hardships to enter the kingdom of God" (Acts 14:22). "Passion and resurrection of the Lord: that is the true Passover," Augustine could write thenceforth,[18] thus concluding the process of Christianizing the ancient Passover and of making it at last and completely embrace both the passion and resurrection of Christ. For until this moment no one had openly explained the term *transitus* as referring to Christ's resurrection.

But a more important synthesis is that between God's Passover and humanity's Passover. How did this synthesis come about in the new definition of the Passover? Here paschal theology sounds the depths of the very person of Christ and fastens upon the mystery of the incarnation. In Jesus, the two Passover protagonists—God and humanity—cease to appear as alternative or juxtaposed entities and become one sole person, since in Christ humanity and divinity are one same person. Author and intended recipient of salvation have met; grace and freedom have kissed each other. The "new and everlasting Covenant" has come to birth: everlasting since henceforth no one can ever again separate the two contracting parties, who have in Christ become one single person.

One doubt remains however to be dispelled: is Jesus then alone in making the Passover? Is it only he who passes from this world to the Father? What about us? Now for the other amazing Augustinian synthesis, the one between the Passover of the Head and the Passover of the body: "There is hope," the passage quoted above continues, "given to the members in their Head, that when he passed they should without doubt follow."[19] Only a hope? More: a fact, even though for the time being only an inchoate one, manifesting itself in faith and the sacraments. "Ever since, as the Apostle wrote, 'he was put to death for our offenses and was raised again for our justification' (Rom 4:25), our own transition from death to life has been consecrated in that passion and resurrection of the Lord."[20] Jesus' passing is not made alone; it is the collective passing of all humanity to the Father. Commenting on the verse in the Psalms which says: "*Singularis ego sum donec transeam*" (Ps 140 [141]:10), "I am *alone* until I have *passed over*," Augustine says that this is the voice of Christ speaking before his Passover, as if to say: "After the Passover I shall no longer be *alone*. Many will follow me, many will imitate me. What does this mean? 'Amen, amen, I say to you, unless a grain

17

of wheat falls to the ground and dies, it remains just a grain of wheat; but if it dies, it produces much fruit.' ''[21] At Christ's Passover, Christ's mystical body the Church was born, a wheat-ear springing from his sepulcher!

All of us have thus already passed, with Christ, to the Father and "our life is hidden with Christ in God" (cf. Col 3:3), although we have yet to pass. *In spe* and *in sacramento*, in hope and by baptism, we have already passed, but we have to pass in the reality of daily life, by imitating Christ's life and particularly his love: "This passing from death to life is wrought in us now by faith, which we have for the pardon of our sins and the hope of eternal life, when we love God and our neighbor."[22]

For pass we must, says Augustine. And if we do not pass to God who remains, we shall pass away with the world that is passing away. But how much happier it is to pass "from the world" than to pass away "with the world"; to pass to the Father, rather than to the Enemy.[23] Passover is to pass to that which will not pass away!

May God, through the merits of Jesus Christ our Head, grant that we may so complete this "holy passage" that at the end we may see his face and be satisfied by his presence forever! Amen.

NOTES

1. Cf. St. Augustine, *Sermo Guelferbytanus* 5.2 (SCh 116, p. 212).
2. *Targum on Exodus* 12:42; cf. also *Pesachim* 10.5.
3. Philo of Alexandria, *De specialibus legibus* 2.145, 147; *De congressu eruditionis gratia* 106.
4. St. Melito of Sardis, *On Pascha* 7 (SCh 123, p. 62).
5. Ibid., 46 (SCh 123, p. 84).
6. St. Dionysius of Alexandria, in Eusebius, *Historia ecclesiastica* 7.22.4.
7. St. Ignatius of Antioch, *Smyrnaeos* 5.3.
8. St. Melito of Sardis, *On Pascha* 66.
9. Cf. Origen, *In Iohannis Evangelium* 10.111 (GCS 4, p. 189).
10. St. Gregory Nazianzen, *Oratio* 45.23 (PG 36, 654).
11. Origen, *In Iohannis Evangelium* 10.110 (GCS 4, p. 189).
12. Gregory of Illiberis, otherwise known as Gregory Baeticus, *Tractatus Origenes* 9.9 (CCL 69, p. 72).
13. Cf. St. Ambrose, *De sacramentis* 1.4.12 (PL 16, 421); *De Cain et Abel* 1.8.31 (PL 14, 332).
14. St. Jerome, *In Matthaeum* 4.26.2 (CCL 77, p. 245).
15. Ambrosiaster, *In epistolas ad Corinthios* 5.7 (CSEL 81, 2, p. 56).

16. St. Augustine, *In Iohannis Evangelium* 55.1 (CCL 36, p. 464).
17. St. Augustine, *Enarrationes in Psalmos* 120.6 (CCL 40, p. 1791).
18. St. Augustine, *De catechizandis rudibus* 23.41 (PL 40, 340).
19. St. Augustine, *In Iohannis Evangelium* 55.1 (CCL 36, 464).
20. St. Augustine, *Epistola* 55.1.2 (CSEL 34, 2, p. 170).
21. St. Augustine, *Enarrationes in Psalmos* 140.25 (CCL 40, p. 2044).
22. St. Augustine, *Epistola* 55.2.3 (CSEL 34, 2, p. 171).
23. Cf. St. Augustine, *In Iohannis Evangelium* 55.1 (CCL 36, p. 464).

Chapter Two

"He Died for Our Sins"

The Paschal Mystery in History (1)

In the previous meditation I attempted to give a general survey of how the paschal concept developed from the Old Testament to the Fathers of the Church. From that rapid sketch it emerged that one event out of all the others eventually imposed itself as the paschal event *par excellence*: that which St. John defines as "the passing of Jesus from this world to the Father." This is the heart of the paschal mystery, the essential point at which the old Passover comes to an end and the new Passover begins, at which the figure ceases and reality comes to be. This event is what we properly call "Christ's Passover," where Christ has value as subject, not as object, and indicates the Passover lived in historic time and in the first person of Jesus himself, during his life on earth.

St. John, I was saying, sums up this paschal nucleus of Christ's life by calling it his passing from this world to the Father. This, however, is no isolated statement in the New Testament but one of a number of synthetic formulations of the so-called paschal mystery, with which we are now trying to deal.

1. *The Paschal mystery*

The best-known formulation of the paschal mystery is the one we find in 1 Corinthians 15:3-4, dating back to no more than half a dozen years after Christ's death, since St. Paul "transmits" it in the form in which he himself had learned it orally shortly after his conversion. Conveniently integrated with Romans 4:25, it runs like this: "Christ died for our sins and was raised for our justification." The structure of this primitive paschal creed is extremely interesting. There are two planes clearly to be distinguished in it: (a) the historical plane, that of the simple facts ("he died," "he

20

was raised"); (b) the religious plane, that of the significance of the facts ("for our sins," "for our justification"). We might call these the plane of the "in itself" and the plane of the "for us." For the Apostle, both of these planes are indispensable for salvation: not only the religious one (the "for me"), but the historical one too. For he says that if Christ had not really been raised from the dead, our faith would be "vain," that is to say, empty (cf. 1 Cor 15:14), precisely because it is faith in an historical event, or in a divine intervention in history, and hence the historical event is its content.

Similarly, the plane of the mystery or of the "for us" is also rooted in history and not merely the fruit of religious interpretation worked up by the post-paschal community. For Jesus, already during his earthly life, especially in instituting the Eucharist, had shown himself to be aware of dying "for the sins of many." And his awareness of this is situated, in some way or other, in history, just as is his awareness of being the Son of God, even if the way in which we find it expressed can be dated to the faith of the post-paschal community. The contrary opinion, which denies Jesus any awareness of the salvific and expiatory significance of his death, is an aberration of the critical school (Reimarus), which only a radically secularized interpretation of Scripture could induce one to accept. It destroys the very soul of the paschal mystery, Jesus' love for his own, which prompts him to give his life for them. The gospel ceases to appear as that which it truly is, that is to say, the gospel of God's love in Christ, if Jesus is made into a pure objectivization, an ignorant and unaware expression, so to speak, of God's love, rather than the supreme subjectivization and personification of the Father's love. This is so true that John, in formulating the paschal mystery, rather than say Jesus died "for our sins," says he died "for love." "Having loved his own in the world, *he loved them to the end*" (John 13:1), and again, "No one has greater love than this: *to lay down one's own life for one's friends*" (John 15:13). But in any case the two things, laying down one's life for sins and laying down one's life for love, are in fact the same thing: "He has loved us and (for this reason) has given himself up for us" (cf. Gal 2:20; Eph 5:2), that is to say, for our sins.

I said that the contrary opinion is the fruit of a radically secularized interpretation of Scripture. It sets out from the presupposition that what actually happened in history can only be known by critical investigation and not by revelation as well. That which is not transmitted by an unbroken chain of written evidence, or which goes beyond opinions current about the Messiah at the time of Jesus, is held to be unhistorical. This ends in the absurdity of denying to the man Jesus that which is normally observed in the lives of the saints: namely, that God could have shown him the purpose of his life and of his decisions by direct revelations. Just as though the Holy Spirit counted for nothing as regards the historical truth of Scripture, as if St. Paul were talking nonsense when he emphatically states that he knows "Christ's mind" (cf. 1 Cor 2:16), or as if the Spirit that revealed the risen Christ's mind to the Apostle could not also reveal the mind of the pre-resurrectional Jesus to him! If it is true that no one "knows what pertains to a person except the spirit of the person that is within" (1 Cor 2:11), it is also true that no one knows the secrets of Christ except the Spirit of Christ who was within him and who then inspired the Scriptures. To today's exegetes who are doing their best to impose "another gospel" on us, one lacking Christ's love and his compassion for our sins, St. Paul might repeat what he said to the Galatians: "If anyone preaches to you a gospel other than the one that you have received, let that one be accursed!" (Gal 1:9).

The paschal faith of Christians thus requires that these three things all be believed at once: first, that Jesus really died and rose again; second, that he died for our sins and rose again for our justification; third, that he died for our sins, knowing that he was dying for our sins; that he died for love, not against his will or by accident.

In this chapter I want to go more deeply into the first aspect of this paschal mystery of death and resurrection: namely, death, "He died for our sins." I will hold consideration of the resurrection till the next chapter.

St. Augustine says, "It is no great thing to believe that Christ died: this the pagans too, and the Jews, and all the wicked believe. This all believe: that he died. Christ's resurrection is what Christians believe in: this we hold a great thing, that we believe that he rose from the dead."[1] By this Augustine does not mean to say that resurrection is more important for us than death, but only that believing in the resurrection of Jesus commits one more, is more comprehensive (anyone who believes that he has risen again also believes that he was dead!) and for this reason more aptly describes the true believer. Similarly, the same holy Doctor says that, of the three things symbolized by the paschal *triduum*— crucifixion, burial, resurrection—the most important one for us, since it concerns us most directly, is that which is symbolized by Good Friday: death. "That of which the cross is the symbol is the business of our present life; those things symbolized by his resurrection we hold by faith and hope."[2]

I do not intend to consider the physical aspect of Jesus' passion so much as the interior and spiritual one: *the death of the heart,* which precedes and gives meaning to the death of the body. It has its culminating moment in Jesus' agony in Gethsemane, when he says, "My soul is sorrowful even to death" (Mark 14:34). The importance of this episode of the redemption is such that we find it preserved in differing forms in three—no less—branches of the New Testament tradition: in the Synoptics, in John (John 12:27: "My soul is troubled now . . .") and in the Epistle to the Hebrews (cf. Heb 5:7-8). Gethsemane signals the deepest depression in the "passing of Jesus from this world to the Father"; it is the "great abyss" mentioned in one of the psalms (Ps 36:7). Meditating on this, we lose that slightly materialistic feeling about the Lord's passion being an ensemble of horrifying torments, or a script written and learned in advance from the Scriptures, which Jesus performs virtually unperturbed. When we approach this mystery we must indeed remove the sandals from our feet, for it is holy; we must be of humble and contrite heart. Woe to those who approach out of curiosity, or merely in a spirit of scholarship. They will be inexorably repulsed; they will believe they have grasped all, yet will have grasped nothing.

I should like to outline an interpretation of this Gethsemane event by using two instruments, dogmatic theology furnishing the first and mystical theology the second.

2. *Gethsemane: a theological explanation*

The Gethsemane experience reaches its climax and resolution in those words of Jesus: "But not what I will but what you will" (Mark 14:36). The theological problem consists entirely in knowing who the "I" is, and who the "you"; who says the *fiat* and to whom it is said.

We know that in ancient times these questions attracted some-what differing answers, depending on the underlying type of Christology. For the Alexandrian school, the "I" who speaks is the person of the Word who, in his incarnate state, says his yes to the divine will (the "you") which he himself has in common with the Father and the Holy Spirit. He who says yes and he to whom he says yes are the same will considered in two different times or two different states: in the state of the incarnate Word and in the state of the eternal Word (for the divine will is one will, common to all three divine persons). The drama (if one may call it that) takes place rather within the heart of God than be-tween God and a human soul; and this is so because the existence in Christ of a free human will has not yet been clearly recognized. This explains why theologians of this school always show a cer-tain embarrassment when dealing with this aspect of Jesus' ex-perience, as also with other analogous aspects (ignorance of the day of the *parousia,* temptations, growth in wisdom, etc.). Some-times, as in Athanasius and Hilary of Poitiers, the experience it-self is rendered null by recourse to the pedagogic explanation, according to which Jesus was not really afraid, did not really weep, was not really ignorant about the day of the *parousia,* but wanted to show himself as being in all things like us, so as to instruct and edify us.

More valid, on this point, is the interpretation of the Antiochene school. The writers of this school perceive a correspondence be-tween what happens in the garden of Gethsemane and what hap-pened in the garden of Eden. If sin consisted initially and always consists essentially in a free act by which the human will disobeys God, the redemption could not but take the form of a human being's return to perfect obedience and submission to God. St. Paul says this clearly: "Just as through the disobedience of one person the many were made sinners, so through the obedience of one the many will be made righteous" (Rom 5:19). But for it to be possible for as perfect an obedience as this to be given, there must be a subject who obeys and a subject who is obeyed: people don't obey themselves! So, who are that "I" and that "you" ringing out in Jesus' words? Why, *the man Jesus* who is obeying *God*! It is the New Adam speaking on behalf of the whole human race; at last he says that free and filial yes to God—for which God in the beginning created heaven and earth and the human race. If salvation lies in obeying God, one can understand how important a place Christ's humanity occupies in the redemption. It is not a merely inert nature, nor is it simply a passive subject, to which one attributes all the things "unworthy of God" which characterize Christ's life; on the contrary, it is an active, free principle, a co-essential agent in the work of our salvation; it is an obedient human being.

But even this compelling interpretation had one serious gap. If Jesus' *fiat* in Gethsemane is essentially the yes of a human being (the *homo assumptus*), even of a human being indissolubly united to the Son of God, how can it have such universal value as to be able "to justify" the entire human race? Jesus appears here more as a sublime model of obedience than as an intrinsic "source of salvation for all who obey him" (Heb 5:9). This is the limitation not only of Antiochene Christology but also of all those modern Christologies according to which the redemptive acts pertain to the "human person" of Jesus, and in which Jesus himself is not clearly acknowledged to be God.

A developing Christology was to fill this gap, thanks principally to the work of St. Maximus the Confessor and the Third Council of Constantinople. St. Maximus asked himself the question: Who is the "I" and who is the "you" in Jesus' prayer in Gethsemane? His reply was very illuminating: it is not Christ's human nature speaking to God (Antiochenes); nor is it God in his incarnate state speaking to himself in his eternal state (Alexandrians). The "I" is the Word, speaking, however, on behalf of the free human will which he has assumed; the "you," on the other hand, is the Trinitarian will which the Word has in common with the Father. In Jesus, the Word (God) humanly obeys the Father! Yet the concept of obedience is not annulled, nor does God obey himself, since between the subject and the end of this obedience there is all the density of a real human nature and of a free human will. He who obeys and he who is obeyed are neither the same will, nor the same person, since he who obeys is the human will of the Word (or the Word in his human will) and he who is obeyed is the divine will common to the entire Trinity.

> For our sake having become like us, as a human being he said to God the Father: "Not mine, but your will be done," since he, who is by nature God, even as a human being had as his will the fulfillment of the Father's will. Consequently, in accordance with both the natures by which and in which and of

which his person was constituted, he revealed himself to be he who naturally wills and works our salvation: on the one hand consenting to this, together with the Father and the Holy Spirit, and on the other becoming obedient to the Father over this, to death, even death on a cross, and himself carrying out, through the mystery of the incarnation, the grand plan for our salvation."[3]

"Humanly, Christ did not will the incarnation, but only divinely with the Father and the Holy Spirit. As regards human consent, the only consent to the incarnation was given by the Virgin Mary. But in Gethsemane, when Jesus says, 'Father, . . . your will be done' (Matt 26:42), he utters the *fiat* of the redemption; now we have the free consent of the human will of a divine person" (M. J. LeGuillou). It was here precisely, as we said before, that grace and freedom kissed and the human and divine Passovers coincided. He who had to fight, that is, human nature, encountered Him who could overcome, that is, God, and victory was the result. For after sin, the human condition can be described thus:

In justice, human nature should have taken up the debt and carried off the victory, but it was enslaved to the very things it would have had to make war on and defeat; God, on the other hand, who could overcome, was not in debt to anyone for anything. Hence, neither the one nor the other joined battle and sin lived on, and it was impossible for true life to become ours, given that the one *ought* to carry off the victory but only the other *could*. This is why it was necessary for the one and the other to unite and for the two natures to come together in one sole being: the nature of him who ought to fight, and the nature of him who could win. And so it falls out: God takes up the struggle on human nature's behalf: human, he as a human being conquers sin, being free, however, of any sin, since he is God."[4]

God obeyed humanly! We understand then what universal saving power is contained in Jesus' *fiat*: it is the human act of a God; it is a divine-human, theandric act. That *fiat* is indeed, to use the words of the psalm, "the rock of our salvation" (Ps 95:1). The salvation of us all rests on it. No one can lay a different foundation from this (cf. 1 Cor 3:11); anyone who meddles with this foundation undermines the very basis of the Christian religion by depriving it of its absolute and universal character.

But let us return for a moment to those words of Jesus: "Not mine, but your will be done." In the mysterious passing-over from that "I" to that "you" is contained the true, definitive, and universal paschal exodus of the human race. This is the crossing of the true Red Sea; a crossing between two shores which are very close together but between which runs an abyss; for we are speaking here about passing from the human will to the divine will, from rebellion to obedience. Following Jesus in this exodus means passing from the old "I" to the new "I," from "me" to other people; from this world to the Father.

3. *Gethsemane: a mystical explanation*

I said that in the passing from "I" to "you" in Jesus' prayer there is an abyss midway. For us to be able to cast a glance into this abyss, the instrument of theological analysis will no longer suffice us; we need that of mystical experience. This alone can give us some inkling of what it cost the Savior to utter his *fiat* and to what in effect he gave his *fiat*. The theological explanation deals with the objective, or ontological, aspect of Jesus' experience, not the subjective and existential one. If what we are talking about in Jesus' case was indeed an experience (not a thing or a line of argument), then plainly to understand it one would need, to some extent, to undergo the same experience oneself. Certain passages in the Bible, as, for instance, that of Gethsemane, or of Jesus' temptations, remain sealed for us unless we can see something similar in the lives of the saints and hence in the life of the Church. Some scholars speculate as to what the source for a narrative like the Gethsemane one, so rich in psychological detail, could be, then only to cast doubt on its historicity, not realizing that what is actually described is virtually nothing: mere pointers, like posts put round a piece of land to warn that, underneath, a chasm yawns. Into that chasm, that abyss, by which I mean Jesus' spiritual agony in Gethsemane, we cannot cast a single glance unless reliving it ourselves or listening to what those mystic souls have said to whom the Lord has granted to relive it at least in part.

The most useful category for approaching the Gethsemane experience is perhaps that of "the dark night of the soul," described by St. John of the Cross. "Since Jesus possesses a human nature and a human will, he also possesses a human subjective center of activity, which is that proper to a creature who freely places himself before the incomprehensible God. This allows Jesus to have the same experiences as we have of God, and in an even more radical, we might almost say, more dreadful way. And this not *in spite* but *because* of the so-called hypostatic union'' (K. Rahner). The actions of Jesus in the olive grove are those of someone prey to mortal anguish: "he knelt down," "he fell face down on the ground," "he stood up to go to his disciples," "he went and prayed again," "he stood up again," "he went to pray again." One thing however is certain: this anguish was not caused by simple foresight of the torments to come. The chalice that dismays him is the chalice of divine wrath, of which it is said that it must be drunk "to the dregs" by sinners (Ps 75:9) or by whoever, as in this case, represents them. Of Jerusalem, punished for her sins, it is said in the prophets that she has drunk "at the LORD's hand the cup of his wrath . . . the bowl of staggering" (Isa 51:17). This chalice is thus the passion, it is true, but not in itself, rather inasmuch as it is the punishment and the fruit of sin.

Seen like this, Jesus' torment seems to be caused by two interdependent facts: the nearness of sin, and the remoteness of God. When in the course of a passive purification God allows a soul a clear sight of its own sinfulness, that soul is filled with deadly terror. Overwhelmed by a mixture of horror, fear, and desperation, it would rather disappear and be annihilated than be confronted with it. Now, Jesus felt sin was near, actually "on his back," and not one or more sins but all the sin in the world. At this point it didn't make any difference that he himself had not committed them; they were his because he had freely taken them on: "He himself bore our sins in his body" (1 Pet 2:24); God "made him to be sin" for our sake (2 Cor 5:21), having become "a curse for us" (Gal 3:13).

Sin's nearness provokes God's remoteness or, more accurately, God's withdrawal as its consequence: the horror of his going away, disappearing, not answering any more. The cry, "My God, my God, why have you forsaken me?" (Matt 27:46)—with what follows in Psalm 22: "far from my prayer, from the words of my cry"—Jesus carried in his heart from Gethsemane onwards. The infinite, loving attraction between Father and Son, is now thwarted by an equally infinite repulsion, since God has an infinite hatred of sin. There are no similes to describe such an experience. If the mere clash in the atmosphere between a cold air current and a hot air current can convulse the sky with terrifying thunderclaps, flashes of lightning, and thunderbolts, what must Jesus' state of soul have been when the supreme holiness of God came in conflict with the supreme malice of sin? In him those words of the psalm were mysteriously fulfilled which say, "Deep [the abyss of holiness] calls to deep [that of sin] in the roar of your cataracts; All your breakers and billows pass over me" (Ps 42:8); "your terrors have cut me off" (Ps 88:17).

After this can we wonder at the cry forced from Jesus' lips, "My soul is sorrowful even unto death," or shall we seek facile explanations for that cry, as some have done in the past? God's holiness makes sin felt for what it is: a deadly danger, like a cry of revolt against the Almighty, the Holy One, Love. God has to distance himself so that sin can grasp what it is and reveal its inner nature through its consequences. When God has totally disappeared, when the creature has "gone down alive into hell" in absolute darkness of spirit, then it understands what it has done by sinning. The soul emerges bruised and martyred from the experience. When the saints describe this kind of experience, they make us shudder. Yet their ordeal is nothing compared to Jesus', who bore the sins of all. "To give some idea of my torments and of my desire to escape from them," wrote the mystic Blessed Angela of Foligno, in connection with one such ordeal, "I say that instead of them I would rather have the ills, maladies, and pains present in all the bodies of all the human beings in the world . . . I would rather endure any type of martyrdom."[5]

The Epistle to the Hebrews says of Jesus that "he learned obedience from what he suffered" (Heb 5:8). What a deep saying! It means that from his Gethsemane experience (for this is what the author is referring to in the context), Jesus above all else experienced what obeying and what disobeying God means. He drank sin's bitter cup to the dregs. And this is why I said at the outset that the paschal mystery is drained of all significance and becomes an empty shell, if we deny that Jesus was aware that he was dying for the sins of the human race.

It is good to stop here and not try to direct our gaze further, but only the heart. Now we know what it cost Jesus to say his *fiat* and to what he gave his *fiat*. He said yes to drinking the cup of God's justice and holiness on behalf of all people. He said yes too to his very real passion, provided we understand his passion not to be the result of accidental and political causes but the result of sin. He said yes, in a word, to fulfilling in himself the destiny of the Servant of Yahweh:

> It was our infirmities that he bore,
> our sufferings that he endured . . .
> But he was pierced for our offenses,
> crushed for our sins.
> Upon him was the chastisement
> that makes us whole (Isa 53:4-5).

The human yes pronounced by a God in the darkness of spirit of his human nature was required to redeem the accumulated rebellion of human beings from the days of Adam onwards. But Jesus really redeemed it with a will!

> By his stripes we were healed . . .
> Because of his affliction he shall see the light . . .
> Through his suffering,
> my servant shall justify many (Isa 53:5, 11).

The Gethsemane experience ends not in defeat but in victory. Jesus descended into hell for us all but did not lose his filial trust in God, whom he continued to call *Abbà*! Daddy! And so his absolute obedience destroyed hell and death, and renewed life. He was truly "heard because of his piety," that is to say because of his obedience (cf. Heb 5:7), and heard beyond anything that could have been foreseen. God bestowed his satisfaction on him in such measure that from him it redounds henceforth on the whole human race: in him all the families of nations are blessed, through his obedience all are "made righteous" (Rom 5:19).

4. *"Whatever is lacking in the obedience of Christ"*

Pascal wrote: "Jesus is in agony in the garden until the end of the world."[6] What he says can be very true if we think of the doctrine of the mystical body. The Head has risen and is glorious, but his body is still on earth enduring trial and tribulation; in a word, it is in agony. But if the body is in agony, He too is, mystically, in agony, for "if one part suffers, all the parts suffer with it" (1 Cor 12:26).

This, however, is not the main point now. The main point is to know what the Jesus who is in agony until the end of the world expects from us. Pascal in that same passage says: one tear of compassion! "Do you want me to go on shedding the blood of my humanity for you, without your sparing a single tear for me?" But this is certainly not the first thing that Jesus expects and wants from us. He wants us to unite with him in obeying the Father; he wants us "to fill up what is lacking in his obedience on behalf of his body, which is the Church" (cf. Col 1:24). "Whoever does the will of God is my brother and sister and mother" (Mark 3:35): that is, the person who is really near me in my agony and comforts me. Each time we are faced with a difficult obedience, we must run and throw ourselves on our knees beside Jesus in Gethsemane and he will teach us how to obey. This way, he will obey in us and with us.

Obedience is the virtue above all of those who rule, of prelates. In them, as in Jesus, shines forth "the essential obedience" which is obeying God. Peter, before the Sanhedrin, said that it is more necessary to obey God than to obey human beings (cf. Acts 4:19). By obeying God, one has the right to be obeyed by human beings. And this is because, in the universe and in the Church, one sole will has to be done, directly or indirectly, by all: that of the heavenly Father.

Obeying God is not an abstract program or meant for only exceptional occasions; on the contrary, it is the daily fabric of Christian existence. Each time we welcome a good inspiration, we are obeying God; each time we say no to the "will of the flesh," we are obeying God. There is no moment, no action, in a believer's life that cannot be transformed into an act of loving obedience to the Father. All we have to do, with a little recollection and concentration, is to ask ourselves: What does the Lord want me to do at this moment, in these circumstances? We know this was what Jesus himself did, so that he could say: "I always do what is pleasing to him" (John 8:29); "My food is to do the will of the one who sent me" (John 4:34).

The greatest joy we human creatures can give God is to share the destiny of Jesus, "Servant of God," by pushing our own will-to-obey to the very limits, even to obeying in the most utter darkness as Jesus did in Gethsemane. Servants of Jesus Christ—those who put their lives totally at God's disposal in Jesus—by virtue of doing so become, like Jesus, the object of the Father's satisfaction. The words once uttered by the Father about Jesus become words uttered for them, above all, those words said to Jesus at his baptism: "You are my beloved son; with you I am well pleased" (Mark 1:11).

I end this meditation with the very familiar words of Philippians 2, which sum up the whole mystery which we have been trying to contemplate. Let us listen to them, not as coming from the mouth of Paul, but as though God the Father were himself proclaiming them:

> Have among yourselves the same attitude *of obedience*
> as was in Christ Jesus, *my Son,*
> who, though he was in the form of God,
> did not regard equality with God
> as something to be grasped.
> Rather, he emptied himself,
> taking the form of a slave,
> coming in human likeness;
> and found human in appearance,
> he humbled himself,
> becoming *obedient to death,*
> even death on a cross.
> Because of this, God greatly exalted him
> and bestowed on him the name
> that is above every name,
> so that at the name of Jesus
> every knee should bend,
> of those in heaven and on earth and under the earth,
> and every tongue confess that
> Jesus Christ is Lord!

NOTES

1. St. Augustine, *Enarrationes in Psalmos* 120.6 (CCL 40, p. 1791).
2. St. Augustine, *Epistola* 55.14.24 (CSEL 34, 2, p. 195).
3. St. Maximus, *In Matthaeum* 26.39 (PG 91, 68).
4. Nicholas Cabasilas, *Vita in Christo* 1.5 (PG 150, 313).
5. *The Book of Bl. Angela of Foligno,* Quaracchi 1985, p. 352.
6. Pascal, *Pensees* 806.

Chapter Three

"He Is Risen Indeed"

The Paschal Mystery in History (2)

1. *"Go and tell Peter . . ."*

"Jesus of Nazareth, the crucified, has risen! Go and tell Peter and the other disciples!" (cf. Mark 16:1-7). Jesus who that Easter morning sent those women to bring the glad news to Peter and his companions now sends me to bring the same tidings to Peter's successor[1] and his companions: He is risen! Jesus of Nazareth, the crucified, is risen!

Subsequently it would be for Peter to carry this news to the whole world. Fifty days later, he would be crying *urbi et orbi,* to the city and to the world, in Jerusalem's main square: "Jesus of Nazareth . . . God has raised him up; of this we are all witnesses" (Acts 2:22, 32). Before this however, someone else, as we have heard, had been charged with taking him the glad news and then disappearing from the scene. This insignificant messenger I should very much like now to be me. I feel, at this moment, like the deacon at the beginning of the Easter Vigil who is preparing to sing the *Exsultet* before the bishop. First he asks a blessing, saying, "Iube domne benedicere: Deign, Father, to bless me." Then he asks for the prayers of all present, saying, "Invoke with me, I beseech you, the mercy of Almighty God, that he who has called me through no merit of mine to be numbered among the Levites, may now grant me to sing this candle's praises by filling me with the grace of its light."

For we need a special grace to talk about Christ's resurrection. We need to be humble, trembling with fear like the holy women, to discharge a task like this. And I know that I am not that kind of person. Even so, I cannot evade the charge received: "Go and tell Peter and the other disciples that I have risen; that they are not to be sad and not to be afraid. Say to the Church: Weep no more; the Lion of the tribe of Judah has triumphed!" (cf. Rev 5:5).

33

I said that we need a special grace to be able to talk about the resurrection. No one can say, "Jesus is Lord," or "Jesus is risen," which is the same thing, except "in the Holy Spirit" (cf. 1 Cor 12:3). Faced with the resurrection, all words fail us. When we pass from proclaiming the cross to proclaiming Christ's resurrection, we are like people who, from dry land, arrive at a run on the seashore. There we are brought up sharp. Our feet are no more use for going further, for walking over the waves. We have to be satisfied with looking out to sea, while staying, with our body, where we are. Who knows what the expression, the look, the voice, the gestures of the women were like when they went into the room and joined Peter and the other apostles? Before they had even opened their mouths, Peter realized something unheard of had occurred and a shudder ran through his whole body; and so it was with everyone else who was there. The numinous suddenly enveloped them, filling the place and all those in it.

That said, it is not hard to imagine what must have happened next. In their excitement, the women were all shouting at once, and the apostles probably had to scold them to make them calm down and say clearly what it was all about. All that could be caught from their bawling were disconnected exclamations with accompanying gestures: "Empty, empty, the tomb is empty! Angels, angels, we have seen angels! Alive, alive, the Master is alive!" This is no rhetorical elaboration on my part; quite the opposite, it is a pale reflection of what actually took place. The news was far greater than the human means available to contain it. It was the new wine bursting the wineskins and pouring out in all directions. Of Christ's resurrection we have to say what is said of the Eucharist in the hymn *Lauda Sion*: "Quantum potes tantum aude; Dare all you can, you have no song worthy his praises to prolong, so far surpassing powers like yours." Would that we too might once experience the resurrection shudder! Would that its numinous charge might take away our speech and fill us, as it is in its nature so to do, with "love and terror," make us "burn and shudder at once," as St. Augustine says.[2]

At the announcement of the resurrection, we ought to shout to ourselves in the words of the psalm: "Awake, O my soul; awake, lyre and harp! I will wake the dawn" (Ps 57:9). But how can we jump for joy, you may ask, when the world is so shaken and disturbed, when "nations are in turmoil and kingdoms totter"? Point taken; but Christ has risen:

Therefore we fear not, though the earth be shaken
and mountains plunge into the depths of the sea,
Though its waters rage and foam
and the mountains quake at its surging . . .
Come! Behold the deeds of the Lord,
the astounding things he has wrought on earth (Ps 46:3-4, 9).

All the "astounding things" that God has done find their fulfillment and more than fulfillment in this astounding thing: the resurrection of Christ. The Risen One entered the upper room "when
the doors were locked"; today too he passes through locked doors.
Through the locked doors of hearts, through the locked doors
of cultures and periods that deny his resurrection, through the
locked doors of atheistic regimes that refuse to acknowledge him
and that fight against him. He has passed, quite recently, through
many of these walls, of which the Berlin Wall was merely symbolic. One of our brother poets, Paul Claudel, devoted these wonderful lines to the resurrection:

Nothing resists this conqueror.
He passes
through locked doors from the other side of the wall.
And thus it is that through the ages
He passes without any breach of rhythm.[3]

Nothing could have stopped its being Easter again this year;
nothing will stop its being Easter a year from now, and so on until
he returns. Nothing can stop the Church from repeating at every
Mass: "We proclaim your death, O Lord, we proclaim your resurrection, until you come in glory."

2. Christ's resurrection and the Paschal mystery

But now the time has come to site the proclamation of the resurrection in the framework of our treatment of the paschal mystery. In what sense does Christ's resurrection form part of the
paschal mystery and in what sense does it, in the paschal mystery, constitute the moment that we call "historical"?

Let us start by answering this second question, which is the
easier of the two. We call Christ's resurrection the "historical"

element in the Christian Passover, not so much as opposed to "unhistorical," that is, something that did not really happen, as opposed to "liturgical," "moral," and "eschatological." In other words, we call it the historical element inasmuch as it represents the unique and unrepeatable event, as distinct from the sacrament, which represents the liturgical aspect and is repeated every year at the feast of Easter and every day in the Eucharist.

The other question is harder to answer: in what sense does the resurrection form part of the paschal mystery, even though this seems so obvious? For we should be aware that what for us today is the primary significance of Easter, namely, Christ's resurrection, was in fact the last to establish itself in the Church's praxis. When this came about, in the fourth to fifth century, it met with resistance. "Some people," we read in a document of the period, "criticize God's Holy Church for applying the name *Pascha* to the venerable feast of Christ our God's resurrection from the dead."[4] When, finally, this usage became general, there were still protests: "Many people," wrote a medieval author, "now only see one thing in Easter (*Pascha*), i.e., that on the first day of the week the Lord rose again, which is why it is also called the Day of the Lord's Resurrection; they forget that Easter primarily signifies that which Christ wrought by his cross and by his blood."[5]

The cause of this difficulty is simple. The resurrection constitutes the absolutely novel element of the Christian Passover, that which was not prefigured, the unexpected. The word *Passover* and the feast itself were not therefore in a state to take this immediately on board. Never in the New Testament does the word *Pascha* designate Christ's resurrection, but only his Passover supper or his sacrifice. True, death and resurrection are seen together and constitute the unique mystery of Christ proclaimed in the *kerygma*. But this mystery of Christ or mystery of salvation is never called "paschal mystery" or Passover mystery. In the second century, people began to say: "The Passover (*Pascha*) is Christ," or rather, "The Paschal mystery is Christ" (Justin, Melito of Sardis). And since in Christ death and resurrection were inseparable, Christ's resurrection gradually came to be comprehended in the word *Passover,* though not without resistance and problems, as we have seen.

The Passover was a pre-existing institution which the Christians inherited from the Old Testament. All its symbolism was directed to immolation, blood, sacrifice. Because this was so, it was easy for Christians to make the transfer to the passion of Christ. The first time the noun is used in its Christian acceptation, in 1 Corinthians 5:7, it indeed means sacrifice, or, preferably, paschal lamb: "Christ our Passover has been sacrificed." When Christianity passed into the Hellenic world, we have seen how the striking similarity between the Hebrew word *pascha* and the Greek word *paschein*, to suffer, led Christians into the error of naively believing that Passover meant passion and of repeating this error for hundreds of years.

The term had originally been explained by the concept of God's "passing over," of skipping, or sparing the houses of the Hebrews (cf. Exod 12:11) but no one could see how this meaning could be applied to Christ; in any case this meaning became lost in the Greek translation of the Bible, with which Christians for the most part were familiar. Also, in New Testament times there had been someone who explained the word *Passover* as *passage* (Philo of Alexandria), but he had interpreted this passage with reference to human beings' passing "from vice to virtue, from sin to grace," which evidently did not apply to Christ.

So for a long while the situation in the Church was this: those who explained *Passover* by *passion* saw the death of Christ prefigured in it; those who explained it in the sense of *passage* saw the crossing of the Red Sea as a figure, not, however, of Christ's resurrection, but of baptism, or the passage of the soul from sin to grace. One has to wait until the fifth century before finding the occasional, rare example where Christ's resurrection is intended by the term passage.[6]

It was Augustine, as we have seen, who made it possible to overcome this difficulty. He discovered that John had given a new interpretation to the term *Passover*: that of Christ's passage "from this world to the Father" (John 13:1). On this basis he was able to extend the concept of Passover to include Christ's resurrection and to formulate the paschal mystery as a mystery of passion and resurrection combined, of death and life, and of passage from death to life. "For by his passion the Lord passed from death to life and made a way for us who believe in his resurrection, so that we too may pass from death to life."[7] "The Lord's passion and resurrection: that is the true Passover!" St. Augustine exclaims elsewhere.[8] "Passover is the day on which we at the same time celebrate the Lord's passion and resurrection."[9] Also, on the plane of faith, Augustine puts Christ's resurrection even above his death, where he writes: "Christ's resurrection is the faith of Christians."[10]

And so death and resurrection together constitute the paschal mystery henceforth. But not as two realities or juxtaposed events, counterbalancing or merely succeeding one another: more truly as a movement, a passage from one to the other. It is dynamic, indicating the profound dynamism of the redemption, which is to make us pass from death to life, from sorrow to joy. More than an event, the Passover is a "becoming," an unstoppable movement. It is a reaching out to the resurrection, it comes about and is only fulfilled in the resurrection. Passover of passion without resurrection would be a question without an answer, a night not ending in the dawn of a new day. It would, in a word, be no beginning at all. So having spoken of Christ's death in the previous chapter, the time has now come to speak about his resurrection and thus complete our treatment of the paschal mystery "in history."

3. *The resurrection of Christ: historical approach*

I explained earlier in what sense we speak of Christ's resurrection as the historical element of the Passover: namely, that it constitutes the "event commemorated," as opposed to the annual liturgical Passover constituting the "commemoration of the event." But is it only in this sense that Christ's resurrection can be called an historical fact? Can we or can we not define the resurrection as an historical event in the more normal sense of the word too, that is to say as having actually happened? In the sense, that is to say, in which historical is opposed to unhistorical, mythical, or legendary? To express ourselves in the terms of the recent debate: Did Jesus rise again only in the *kerygma* and liturgy of the Church, or did he actually rise from the dead in fact and in history? Did he rise again because the Church believes he did and proclaims he did, or did he rise again and hence the Church proclaims him resurrected? Again: did the *person* of Jesus rise again, or was it only his *cause*, in the purely metaphorical sense in which rising again means the survival or the victorious reemergence of an idea after the death of the person who put it forward?

The most authoritative answer is already to be found in the gospel, put there in anticipation by the Holy Spirit: "He has truly been raised," say the apostles as they welcome the two disciples back from Emmaus, even before the latter can recount their own experience (cf. Luke 24:34). So, he has risen "in actual fact," "truly" (*ontos*). The oriental Christians have made this sentence their Easter greeting: "The Lord is risen," to which the response is, "He is risen indeed!"

So let us see where an historical approach to Christ's resurrection will take us. Not because some of us still do not believe in it or need to be persuaded by this means, but, as St. Luke says at the beginning of his Gospel, "so that we may realize the certainty of the teachings which we have received" (cf. Luke 1:4).

With the passion and death of Jesus, the light that had been kindled in the souls of the disciples could not stand up to the ordeal of his tragic end. The most absolute darkness fell once more on all. They had been near to recognizing him as the one sent by God, as someone who was greater than all the prophets. Now they don't know what to think. Luke describes their state of mind for us in the episode of the two disciples at Emmaus: "We were hoping that he would be the one . . . but three days have gone by now" (cf. Luke 24:21). They have reached the nadir of faith and reckon the case of Jesus to be closed.

Now—still in our capacity as historians—let us pass on a few years. What do we find? A group of people, the same ones as had been close to Jesus, who are going about, repeating by word of mouth and in writing that Jesus of Nazareth was himself the Messiah, the Lord, the Son of God; that he is alive and that he will come to judge the world. The case of Jesus has not only been reopened but in no time at all has acquired incredibly deep and universal dimensions. The man affects not only the Jewish people but all people of all time. "The stone which the builders rejected," says St Peter, "has become the cornerstone" (1 Pet 2:7), the beginning of a new humanity. Henceforth there is no other name under heaven given to human beings by which we can be saved, except that of Jesus of Nazareth (cf. Acts 4:12).

What has happened in the meanwhile? What has caused so radical a change that the same people who had repudiated Jesus and run away now say these things publicly, found Churches in Jesus' name and calmly allow themselves to be imprisoned, scourged, and killed for his sake? In chorus, they give us this answer: "He is risen!'' The last act that the historian can perform before yielding the word to faith is to verify this answer, to go, like the holy women, to the tomb and see how things stand.

The resurrection is an historical event in one very special sense. It is at the boundary of history, like a line dividing the sea from dry land. It is simultaneously in it and outside it. With it, history opens on to that which is beyond history: eschatology. In a certain sense therefore it is the rupture and conquest of history, just as the creation is the beginning of history. This makes the resurrection an event which in itself cannot be evidenced or grasped with the mental categories we have, since these are bound up with experience in time and space. For no one was present at the instant when Jesus rose again. No one can claim to have seen Jesus rising again, but only to have seen him once he had risen. The resurrection is thus known a posteriori, afterwards, exactly like the incarnation inside Mary's womb. The physical presence of the Word in Mary's womb is what demonstrates the fact that the incarnation has taken place; similarly, it is the spiritual presence of Christ in the community, made visible by his appearances, that demonstrates that he has risen. This explains why no profane historian mentions the resurrection. Tacitus, who merely records the death of a certain Christus in the days of Pontius Pilate,[11] says nothing about the resurrection. That event had neither relevance nor meaning except for those who experienced its effects within the primitive Christian community.

In what sense then are we talking of an historical approach to the resurrection? What offer themselves to historical consideration and empower the historian to speak of the resurrection are two facts: first, the unforeseen and inexplicable faith of the disciples, a faith so tenacious as to hold firm even under the trial of martyrdom; second, the explanation left us for this faith by the parties involved, that is, the disciples. ''In the decisive moment, when Jesus had been captured and put to death, the disciples harbored no expectation of a resurrection. They ran away, reckoning the case of Jesus to be closed. Something therefore must have happened shortly afterwards which not only caused the radical change in their state of mind but also spurred them to totally new activity and the founding of the Church. This 'something' is the historical nucleus of the Easter faith.''[12]

Let us therefore examine the testimony of the apostles and see how close to the resurrection event this will allow us to get.

The earliest testimony is that of Paul and it goes like this:

> For I handed on to you as of first importance what I also received: that Christ died for our sins in accordance with the Scriptures; that he was buried; that he was raised on the third day in accordance with the Scriptures; that he appeared to Kephas, then to the Twelve. After that, he appeared to more than five hundred brothers at once, most of whom are still living, though some have fallen asleep. After that he appeared to James, then to all the apostles. Last of all, as to one born abnormally, he appeared to me (1 Cor 15:3-8).

These words were written in A.D. 56 or 57. The central nucleus of the text, however, consists of an earlier creed which St. Paul says he had himself received from others. Bearing in mind that Paul learned formulae like this immediately after his conversion, we can date these back to about A.D. 35, that is to say, to half a dozen years after Christ's death. Very ancient testimony indeed.

But what, concretely, do these formulae attest? Two fundamental facts: that "he was raised" and that "he appeared."

"He was raised" (in Greek: *egegertai*), in the sense of "he came back to life," "he rose again," or, in the passive, "he was brought back to life," "resuscitated," by God the Father, are certainly inadequate means of expression. For Christ does not come *back* to life, to his old life, like Lazarus, to die all over again sometime later; he comes *forward* to life in a new world, to the new life according to the Spirit. We are speaking of something for which there is no analogy in human experience and hence which has to be expressed in inappropriate and figurative terms. Christ's resurrection is something completely different from all known resurrections from death, including those wrought by Jesus himself during his life on earth. These are only a postponement or a delaying of death; that however is the definitive and irreversible victory over death.

"He appeared" (in Greek: *ophthe*), in the sense that he showed himself, was made visible by God. From this word we can only deduce that the witnesses were convinced that the Crucified whom they had left on Golgotha and he who subsequently appeared were the same person. This was evidently a very powerful, very concrete experience, of which "it is impossible for us not to speak"

(Acts 4:20). Those who experienced this were certain they had met him, Jesus of Nazareth in person, not a ghost. Paul says most of them were still alive, thus tacitly suggesting that the reader who wanted to be sure on this point should go and consult them. What others had experienced was confirmed by his own experience: "he also appeared to me."

THE TESTIMONY OF THE GOSPELS

The gospel narratives reflect a later phase in the Church's thought, showing editorial divergences and apologetic aims. But the central nucleus of the testimony remains unchanged: the Lord has risen and has appeared alive. To this a new element is added: the empty tomb. From it, John draws a sort of physical proof of Jesus' resurrection (John 20:3f.): the burial cloths on the ground and the headcloth rolled up elsewhere, as though the body had evaporated. The fact of the empty tomb could have several explanations and it never formed the basis for faith in the resurrection. Later, to counteract the story put about by enemies that the body had been stolen, other new elements were stressed in support of the fact: the angels, the story that the guards had been corrupted by the Jewish leadership, etc.

For the Gospels as for Paul, the apparitions were still the decisive factor. The apparitions, however, also witness to the new dimension of the Risen One, his mode of existence "according to the Spirit" which is new and different from his earlier mode of existence "according to the flesh." For instance, he can be recognized, not by anyone who sees him, but only by those to whom he chooses to make himself known. His body is constituted differently from before. He is free of physical law: he comes in and goes out through locked doors; he appears and disappears. Where did Jesus go when he disappeared, where did he reappear from? For us, this is a mystery, as too his eating after the resurrection is a mystery. We lack any experience at all of the world to come, into which he had passed, which would allow us to talk about this.

THE RESURRECTION, OBJECTIVE OR ONLY SUBJECTIVE EVENT?

A different explanation of the resurrection, proposed not long ago by R. Bultmann, involves psychogenic visions, that is, subjective phenomena. But this, were it true, would ultimately constitute no less a miracle than the one he seeks to avoid having to admit. For it supposes that different people in different situations and places have all had the same impressions, or hallucinations. The disciples were not likely to be deceived: they were hard-headed people, fisher-folk, not at all the type who tend to have visions. To begin with, they do not believe; Jesus has as it were to overcome their resistance: "O slow of heart to believe!" Nor could they want to deceive others. All their interests were opposed to this; they would have been the first to be, and to feel, let down by Jesus. If he had not risen again, what was the point of risking persecution and death for him?

The demythologization theory advances a basic objection to the fact of the resurrection as it is related by the witnesses of those days: This claim reflects the way of thinking and of picturing the world in a pre-scientific age, which conceived of the universe as made up of three planes—God, human beings, and the underworld—with the possibility of passing from one to another. This is a mythological concept of the world which today is outdated. Demythologization has had its truths and uses, but it cannot be applied to the specific case of the resurrection, as has been done. For resurrection from death, as the Gospels mean it (i.e., of soul and body), conflicted with the ancient conception of the world, particularly for the Greeks, just as much as it conflicts with ours today. If therefore the apostles defended it so tenaciously, this was not because it conformed to the notions of their day but because it was the truth. Furthermore, it is easy to demonstrate the inconsistency of Bultmann's explanation even within the framework of his theory. He admits that God intervened in the case of Jesus Christ, endorsing his cause. It is clear therefore that in a certain way God acted miraculously in Jesus of Nazareth. But if he acts miraculously, what difference does it make to admit the fact of real resurrection and real appearances, as opposed to facts interior and purely visual? Why did God need to have recourse to an apparent miracle when he could have worked a real one?

The truth of the matter is that beneath the denial of the reality or historicity of the resurrection is an implicit denial of the reality of the incarnation. For Bultmann, the formula, "Christ is God" is false in any sense when "God is considered as objective being; it is correct if 'God' is meant as the event of divine actuation"[13] But if the incarnation is not objective, it is clear that neither can the resurrection be so. The problem is therefore up-stream. The entire diatribe about the reality of the resurrection turns on an ambiguity. The real problem is the divinity of Christ. It is about knowing who Jesus Christ is. Those who deny the reality of the resurrection are consistent with themselves, even if they are not consistent with Scripture and dogma. The same arguments which are advanced against the possibility of the resurrection could also be advanced against the incarnation. The Fathers were not mistaken in treating incarnation and resurrection in close relationship, and in demonstrating the one by the other. As the Word came into the world without violating his mother's virginity, so he entered the Upper Room through locked doors. Can one admit a real incarnation and hypostatic union as defined by the ancient Councils and professed by Christians in their creed, and yet deny the resurrection? The collapse of the faith, in this case, would not stop merely at the incarnation but would also inexorably take away the Trinity, since we only know the Son by virtue of the incarnation.

The historical character, that is to say the objective and not merely subjective character, of the resurrection once denied, the birth of the Church and the faith becomes a more inexplicable mystery than the resurrection itself. This same author who denies any relevance to the historical Jesus and would have all Christianity depend on the paschal experience of the apostles, then empties this paschal experience of all content by making it something interior and more or less visionary. "The assumption that the whole great course of Christian history is a massive pyramid balanced upon the apex of some trivial occurrence is surely a less probable one than that the whole event, the occurrence *plus* the meaning inherent in it, did actually occupy a place in history at least comparable with that which the New Testament assigns to it."[14]

What, then, is the end-point of historical research about the resurrection? We may gather what it is from the words of the disciples at Emmaus: Some of the disciples had gone to Jesus' tomb on Easter morning and found things were as the women described who had been there before them, "but him they did not see." So history goes to Jesus' tomb and has to confirm that things are as the witnesses have said. But him, the Risen One, history cannot see. It is not enough to establish him historically; we need

44

to see him, and this is not granted to history, but only to faith.[15] In any case, it was the same for the witnesses of those days. They too had to make the leap. From the apparitions and, perhaps, from the empty tomb, which are historical facts, they came to the affirmation: "God has raised him up," which is an affirmation of faith. As an affirmation of faith, it is more than a conquest; it is a gift. For in the gospel we see that not all saw the Risen One, but only those to whom he chose to make himself known and when he chose to make himself known. The Emmaus disciples had walked beside him without recognizing him until, when he chose and when their hearts were ready to accept the grace, "their eyes were opened and they recognized him" (Luke 24:31).

4. *The resurrection of Christ; a faith approach*

The resurrection of Christ is like a mountain peak that acts as a watershed; in one direction it faces towards history and leads to history; in the other, it faces towards faith and leads to faith. Let us now come down in the opposite direction from the one in which we came; let us follow the crest of faith. By passing from history to faith, our way of talking about the resurrection changes too; our tone, our language. We do not adduce proofs and confirmations; there is no need for them, for the voice of the Spirit creates conviction directly within the heart. It is an assertive, apodictic language. "But now Christ has been raised from the dead" (1 Cor 15:20), says St. Paul. Now we are on the plane of faith, no longer on that of demonstration. It is the *kerygma:* "Scimus Christum surrexisse a mortuis vere," runs the liturgy for Easter Day: "We know that Christ has really risen." This too is the language of faith. Not only do we believe but, having believed, we know that it is so, we are sure of it. We are talking about a certainty different in nature from the historical kind, yet stronger since founded on God. Only the unbeliever or the agnostic can regard this as the arrogant claim of people who believe themselves to be in possession of the truth and refuse all further discussion. In fact, it is the language of those who are totally submitted, as a result of practicing what St. Paul calls "the obedience of faith" (Rom 1:5).

45

The importance of Christ's resurrection for the faith is such that without it, says St. Paul, our faith would be "empty," that is to say baseless, without historical foundation (1 Cor 15:14). We believe in him who has raised Jesus Christ from the dead (Rom 4:24). Now we can understand why St. Augustine could say that "Christ's resurrection is what Christians believe in." That Christ died everyone believes, including the pagans; that he has risen only Christians believe and people who do not believe it are not Christians.[16]

But what is the resurrection, considered from the standpoint of the faith? It is God's testimony about Jesus Christ. Let us read the first sermon on the resurrection, preached by St. Peter to the people of Jerusalem immediately after Pentecost: "You who are Israelites, hear these words. Jesus the Nazorean was a man commended to you by God with mighty deeds, wonders and signs . . . you killed, using lawless men to crucify him. But God raised him up . . . Of this we are all witnesses" (Acts 2:22-32).

Here we have one concept of testimony: that which the apostles render to Jesus' resurrection. The entire New Testament is full of this. But there is another testimony too: that which God has rendered to Jesus Christ by raising him up. God who had already commended Jesus of Nazareth with wonders during his life, has now set a final seal on acknowledging him: he has raised him from the dead. St. Paul in his sermon to the Athenians formulates the matter like this: "God has provided confirmation for all by raising him from the dead" (Acts 17:31). "Confirmation," sure proof, of what precisely? Of the truth of Jesus Christ, the authenticity of his person and of his mission. God guarantees that Jesus of Nazareth is indeed who he said he was. The resurrection is God's potent yes, his amen pronounced on the life of Jesus.

Is not Christ's death in itself already sufficient testimony? No. It is not sufficient to establish the truth of his cause. Many people on earth have died for mistaken causes, even for unjust causes. Their deaths did not make their causes any better; they merely testified that they personally believed these causes to be just. "So, the noble testimony that Jesus Christ gave before Pontius Pilate" (cf. 1 Tim 6:13) is not the testimony of his genuineness, but only testimony of his love: the supreme such testimony, since "no one has greater love than this, to lay down one's life for one's friends" (John 15:13).

Only the resurrection constitutes the seal of Christ's divine authenticity. That is why Jesus himself points to it as the sign *par excellence*. To people who asked him for a sign, Jesus replied: "Destroy this temple and in three days I will raise it up" (John 2:18f.). Paul is right therefore to take the resurrection as foundation for building the entire structure of faith: "If Christ had not been raised, our faith would have been vain. We should also have been false witnesses to God. . . . We should be the most pitiable people of all" (cf. 1 Cor 15:14-15, 19).

What, then, does the fact that he has risen concretely attest about Christ? First, it points us to the earthly person and work of Jesus: the historical Jesus, who "went about doing good and healing everyone," whom people killed by hanging him on a cross, whom God raised to life on the third day (cf. Acts 10:38f.). On the cross, God seemed to have disavowed Jesus, to the point of wringing from him that anguished cry: "God, my God, why have you forsaken me?" But now, by bringing him back to life, the Father shows that he identifies himself with the Crucified and his cause. Henceforth it will be impossible to see the Crucified otherwise than "in the glory of the Father" and the Father's glory otherwise than in the countenance of the Crucified. Thus the resurrection is like a lighthouse focusing back beyond his Passover onto the earthly life of Jesus. By its light the disciples remembered, understood, and fixed the words and deeds performed by Jesus, above all that last mysterious deed when, taking bread, he broke it and gave it to them, saying, "Take this, all of you, and eat it: this is my body which will be given up for you."

The very words uttered by Jesus during his life (later to be collected together in the gospel) are raised to a new state by the resurrection. They become freed from their time limitations and acquire universal absoluteness. No longer just sapiential or prophetic teaching, they can be seen for what they are: "words that do not pass away," the Word of God.

During his life Jesus had proclaimed: "The kingdom of God is at hand!" This was the core of his proclamation. The resurrection attests to us that he was not mistaken: with him, dead and risen again, the kingdom of God has come. The end has already begun: never mind when it will finish, whether in a matter of years as the earliest witnesses thought, or in thousands and millions of years.

Seen from the standpoint of faith, however, the resurrection is not only this. To this significance, which we might call *apologetic* since it tends to establish the authenticity of Christ's mission and the legitimacy of his divine claim, we must add a completely different one, which we may call *mystical* or salvific and which has only recently received the attention it deserves. The resurrection not only proves the *truth* of Christianity but is also the foundation of the Christian *reality*. It is an integral part of the mystery of salvation.

For some people the resurrection does not seem to mark a new and real intervention by God in history, any different from the cross. Its salvific significance only consists in revealing the inner meaning of the cross (thus Bultmann). But this is certainly not enough. St. Paul stresses the specific significance of the resurrection when he derives justification itself (cf. Rom 4:25) and the remission of sins (1 Cor 15:17) from it. There is more at issue here than an example, in the sense that the death and resurrection of Christ are the model, the paradigm of death to sin and of new life in God, and of our own death and resurrection. The schema "*as with* Christ, *so with* us" (cf. Rom 6:4f.) also means "*because with* Christ, *therefore with* us too." Because Christ died, we have died to sin; because Christ has risen, we can walk in newness of life. Christ has risen for our justification, that is to say, to cause it and not merely to point the way to it. St. Augustine has expressed all this perfectly, rightly linking it to the act of faith in the resurrection: "By his passion the Lord passed from death to life and made a way for us who *believe* in his resurrection, so that we too may pass from death to life."[17] He does no more than take up St. Paul's teaching: "If you believe in your heart that God raised him from the dead, you will be saved" (Rom 10:9).

It is significant that only after the resurrection does Jesus call his disciples "brothers." "Go to my brothers and tell them, 'I am going to my Father and your Father'" (John 20:17). No longer only slaves, no longer only friends (cf. John 15:15), he is not ashamed to call them brothers since "he who consecrates and those who are being consecrated all have one origin" (Heb 2:11-12).

As from the incarnation we had "the same flesh" in common with Christ, so from the resurrection we also have "the same Spirit" in common with him. For with the resurrection Jesus has become "a life-giving Spirit" (1 Cor 15:45).

CONCLUSION: A PURER FAITH

Everything that has been said only reaffirms, in more modern words, the Church's traditional faith concerning the resurrection. Has all the recent discussion aroused by rationalistic criticism and demythologizing theory been a waste of time? By no means. It has brought a purification of the faith, which was needed in order for faith to be restated today. It has liberated belief in the resurrection from representations by turns distinctly crude and falsely apologetic. In order to stress the reality and the historicity of the resurrection, we have often ended up presenting it as a material, verifiable event, a fact of experience rather than of faith. On the contrary, of the resurrection as of Christ's divinity, we are not granted direct but only indirect knowledge, the result of the leap of faith. This whole challenge helps us to be more sober in our religion, more humble and more silent before the divine and the ineffable. It has made our faith more naked and therefore purer, like a kind of "dark night of the senses," through which the faith of the whole Church has passed or must pass.

But the usefulness of the challenge has not only been negative. There is an extraordinarily comforting thrill in the affirmation that Jesus has risen, in the *kerygma*, once we have established that he rose in history too. If Christ rises again in the *kerygma*, when it is proclaimed with faith by the Church, then he is forever in the act of rising again. He wishes to rise again this Easter and waits for us to make him rise again by preaching his resurrection "in the Spirit."

He has risen, perhaps this very moment, here among us, and blessed are they who can now say, like St. Paul, "He has appeared to me too" (cf. 1 Cor 15:8).

NOTES

1. This meditation, like the other ones, was first delivered in the presence of the Pope.

49

2. Cf. St. Augustine, *Confessions* 7.16; 11.9.
3. Paul Claudel, *La nuit de Pâques* (Easter Night) in *Oeuvre Poétique* (Paris, 1967) p. 826.
4. *Chronicon Paschale,* ed. L. Dindorf, Bonn 1832, vol. 1, p. 424.
5. Rupert of Deutz, *De divinis officiis* 6.26 (CCLM 7, p. 207).
6. Cf. St. Maximus of Turin, *Sermo* 54.1 (CCL 23, p. 218); Ps. Augustine, *Sermo Caillau-St. Yves* 1.30 (PLS 2, 962).
7. St. Augustine, *Enarrationes in Psalmos* 120.6 (CCL 40, p. 1791).
8. St. Augustine, *De catechizandis rudibus* 23.41.3 (PL 40, 340).
9. St. Augustine, *Sermo Denis 7* (*Miscellanea Agostiniana,* 1, p. 32).
10. St. Augustine, *Enarrationes in Psalmos* 120.6 (CCL 40, p. 1791).
11. Tacitus, *Annals* 25.
12. M. Dibelius, *Jesus,* Berlin, 1966, p. 117.
13. Cf. R. Bultmann, *Glauben und Verstehen,* 2, Tübingen 1938, p. 258.
14. Ch. H. Dodd, *History and the Gospel,* London 1964, 76.
15. Cf. S. Kierkegaard, *The Journals* 10:4 A, entry 523.
16. Cf. St. Augustine, *Enarrationes in Psalmos* 120.6 (CCL 40, p. 1791).
17. Ibidem.

Chapter Four

"Do This in Memory of Me"

The Paschal Mystery in the Liturgy (1)

In the two foregoing chapters I presented Christ's Passover, that is, his passing from this world to the Father, through the abyss of his passion and through his resurrection. Christ's Passover is prolonged and perpetuated in the Church in two ways, or on two planes, each distinct from, even though intimately connected with, the other. The first is the plane of liturgy and community, which we might call the *objective* plane, or again the mysterial plane, since it takes place principally in the "mysteries," the sacraments. To this plane belong, as well as the annual feast of Easter, the sacraments of baptism, of the Eucharist, and of reconciliation insofar as this last is also a paschal sacrament. The second is the existential and personal plane, which we might describe as the *subjective* plane, or again the moral plane, since it takes effect through the Christian's moral and ascetic efforts. To this second plane belongs teaching on conversion, on purification, and, generally, what the Fathers define as "the passing from vice to virtue, from sin to grace."

There is, therefore, a paschal mystery that is celebrated in the liturgy and a paschal mystery that occurs in life. They are inseparable: the Passover of the liturgy has to nourish the Passover of life, and the latter authenticates the former.

These two Passovers—which we may call "The Church's Passover" and "our Passover" respectively—have a common basis without which what they signify cannot operate effectively, and this common basis is *faith*. St. Paul says: "If you confess with your mouth that Jesus is Lord and believe in your heart that God raised him from the dead, you will be saved" (Rom 10:9). This is the equivalent of saying: if you believe in Christ's Passover, you too will make your Passover. St. Augustine makes this point very clearly: "By his passion the Lord 'passed' from death to life and made a way for us who *believe* in his resurrection, so that

51

we too may 'pass' from death to life."[1] One of the Greek Fathers expresses the same thought in surprisingly modern and existential terms: "Anyone who knows the Passover to have been sacrificed for him, may consider that life begins for him from the moment Christ has been sacrificed for him. However, Christ is sacrificed for him the moment he recognizes grace and becomes aware of the life procured for him by such a sacrifice."[2]

Faith, a living, personal faith not only in the actual event of Christ's death and resurrection, but also in the significance this event has for me, *hic et nunc*, is thus the obligatory approach, a sort of entrance gate, to the light of the Passover. *Lumen Christi!* "Light of Christ!" the cry rings out at a certain point in the liturgy for the Easter vigil. As, in the natural order, it is not sufficient for the light to shine, but one's eyes must be open to see it, so, in the spiritual order, one must have faith if one is to see and rejoice in the Sun of Righteousness as he rises again from the underworld.

After this preamble we shall consider the two Passovers separately, devoting two chapters to the paschal mystery in the liturgy and two to the paschal mystery in life.

As far as its essential nucleus is concerned, the liturgical Passover or Passover of the Church is based on the will of Jesus, who instituted the paschal sacraments and the Eucharist in particular, saying, "Do this in memory of me" (Luke 22:19). Here the Christian Passover follows in the wake of the Jewish one. As the Passover liturgy of Israel commemorated the historical Passover of the Exodus, so the Passover liturgy of the Church commemorates the factual Passover of Jesus, that is to say his passing from this world to the Father. Thus the feast of the Passover runs right through salvation history from end to end, constituting a kind of backbone and guiding thread.

In this chapter I shall consider three aspects of the Church's liturgical Passover, as these can be gathered from the great tradition of the Fathers: the liturgical, the theological, and the spiritual. In the first, I shall sketch the development of the paschal ceremonies; in the second, I shall deal with the soteriological significance of Easter; in the third, I shall discuss how to make Easter the occasion for a personal encounter with the Risen Lord.

1. *The ritual development of Easter*

As regards ceremonies, from the origins until towards the end of the fourth century, the Church's Passover was a very simple affair. Everything revolved round the paschal vigil, which was celebrated on the night between the Saturday and Sunday (for the Quartodecimans, on the night between 13 and 14 Nisan), preceded by one or two days of fasting. It began at sunset and finished the next morning, at cockcrow, with the celebration of the Eucharist. During the vigil, baptism was administered, passages from the Bible were read, among which invariably was Exodus 12 (which today, however, has vanished from the vigil!), hymns were sung, and the bishop delivered the homily. In this earliest period, even the vigil, like the whole of Easter, had a Christological rather than a moral or ascetic content. It was, quite literally, "a vigil for the LORD" (Exod 12:42) and not a vigil for human beings. What "vigil for the LORD" actually means is explained in masterly fashion by St. Chromatius of Aquileia in this discourse for Easter Eve:

> All vigils that are celebrated in honor of the Lord are pleasing and acceptable to God; but this vigil is above all vigils. It is called "the vigil for the Lord" *par excellence*. For it is written, "This is the vigil for the Lord, and all Israelites must keep it" (Exod 12:42). With good reason is tonight called the "vigil for the Lord"; for he kept vigil in his lifetime, so that we should not fall asleep in death. In the mystery of the passion, he underwent the sleep of death for our sake, but this sleep of the Lord's has become the whole world's vigil, since Christ's death has banished the sleep of eternal death from us. And this is what he himself says through the prophet: "After that, I lay down to sleep and woke up again and my sleep had grown sweet to me" (cf. Ps 3:6; Jer 31:26). Truly, that sleep of Christ's has become sweet since it has recalled us from bitter death to sweet life. Lastly, tonight is called the "vigil for the Lord," because he wakens from his own sleep of death. That is what he means when he himself says through the mouth of Solomon: "I sleep but my heart keeps vigil" (Cant 5:2), alluding openly to the mystery of his divinity and of his flesh. He slept in the flesh but kept vigil in his divinity, which could never sleep. Of Christ's divinity we read: "The guardian of Israel neither slumbers nor sleeps" (Ps 121:4). This, therefore, is why he said: "I sleep but my heart keeps vigil." For in his sleep of death he slept accord-

53

ing to the flesh, but with his divinity he patrolled the infernal regions, to snatch forth Adam who was imprisoned in them. Our Lord and Savior willed to visit every part, so as to take pity on all. From heaven he came down to earth to visit the world; from earth he then descended into hell to bring light to those who were shut up in hell, as the prophet says: "A light has risen for you who sit in darkness and in the shadow of death" (cf. Luke 1:78-79; Isa 9:1). It is right therefore that this night, in which he brought light not only to this world but also to those who were among the dead, should be called the "vigil for the Lord."[3]

The paschal vigil, as we see, is the "vigil for the Lord" in two senses: in the sense that the Lord's sleep of death procured the awakening, or life, for us all; and in the sense that while his human nature "slept" in death, his divine nature (his heart!) kept vigil, that is, was alive. The paschal mystery is seen, once again, to be anchored on the Christological mystery, on the structure of the person of Christ, human being and God. Since Christ was both divine and human, he could sleep and watch, that is to say be dead *and* alive, at the same time: to sleep as human being and watch as God, to suffer death as human being and as God to confer life.

I mentioned the bishop's homily. This was an abridgement of all salvation-history and more particularly of the whole life and mystery of Christ, from his incarnation to his ascension into heaven. It is easy to grasp why this should have been so. During this period there were no feasts in the year except Easter; not even Christmas, which appears at the beginning of the fourth century. Everything was concentrated on Easter. Easter was a synthetic celebration, in the sense that all the paschal events were celebrated at once, in their dialectical unity of death-life, as a single mystery, inclusively.

From the fourth century, this synthetic celebration is replaced by an analytical or historicized celebration, a celebration that distributes the events by celebrating them each on the day when historically they occurred (the institution of the Eucharist on Maundy Thursday, the passion on the Friday, the resurrection on the Sunday, the ascension on the fortieth day, and so forth). In a short while we witness the transition from the "Easter feast" to the "paschal cycle" consisting, before Easter, of Lent, Holy

Week, the paschal Triduum and, after Easter, of the Octave, the Ascension, and Pentecost.

This kind of fragmentation of the unitary feast into a number of feasts related to one another undoubtedly corresponded to the need for a greater length of time over which to distribute the rich content of Easter and to impart a complete pre-baptismal and mystagogic catechesis to the catechumens and neophytes. However, the process was also favored by an external factor: the spread throughout Christendom of the ceremonies in use in Jerusalem, where the pilgrims loved to recall every detail of Jesus' passion at the spot and the exact moment at which it had originally taken place. The paschal vigil long preserved its central position as a unitary celebration of the whole mystery of death and resurrection and of waiting for the coming of Christ. With the passing of time, however, the tendency to distribute and dilute the contents of the feast into a number of ceremonies on different days detracted from Easter itself, depriving it of much of the primitive force that had come from its great theological concentration.

2. *The theological significance of Easter*

While this evolution of paschal rites was going on, largely due to a spontaneous, creative process at work throughout Christendom, theology for its part developed an intense preoccupation with the nature of the rites, that is to say with the actual nature of the liturgical action. The achievements of the Fathers in this sphere molded all the Church's subsequent sacramental theology, the spiritual afflatus and concrete quality of which have not, truth to tell, always been very happily maintained. It is to these achievements, therefore, that we must always return whenever we wish to renew and re-enliven Christian worship in depth, rather than to the later speculations of commentators on the Fathers, even though these too cannot, of course, be ignored.

I mentioned the theological preoccupation the Fathers developed with the nature of Christian worship. I shall now try to give a résumé of their teaching, assembling it around two basic questions: what is the relationship between liturgy and history? and what is the relationship between liturgy and grace?

The relationship between liturgy and history. The problem can also be stated in the following terms: what is the relationship between the Church's Passover and Christ's Passover? The Church's Passover, it has been said, "prolongs" and "perpetuates" Christ's Passover through the centuries; but this is too vague and general an answer. What does "prolong" mean and how does it actually work? This is basically the same problem posed in our own times over the relationship between the sacrifice of the cross and the sacrifice of the Mass, which assumes so much importance in ecumenical dialogue with Protestants.

Augustine says in one of his deepest and finest paschal homilies:

> We know, my brothers, and we hold it in very firm faith that Christ died one sole time for us: the Just One for sinners, the Master for slaves. . . . As the Apostle says: "He was delivered up for our sins, and rose again for our justification" (Rom 4:25). You know very well that all this only happened once. Yet, the solemnity periodically renews it, as if that were happening again which (historical) truth, in so many places in Scripture, declares has happened only once. Nevertheless, truth and the solemnity are not at variance, in the sense that one is lying and the other telling the truth. As a matter of fact, what truth declares has actually happened only once, this the solemnity renews as worthy of being often celebrated by pious hearts. Truth reveals what has happened as it actually took place; the solemnity however, not by re-enacting events but by dwelling on them, does not permit the past to pass away. In a word, "Christ, our Passover, has been sacrificed" (1 Cor 5:7). Though he died once, "he dies no more; death no longer has power over him" (Rom 6:9). Therefore, according to this voice of truth, we say that our Passover victim has been sacrificed once and that he will not die again; nevertheless, according to the voice of the feast, we say that the Passover will return every year. . . . To this reasoning we owe the glorious celebration of this night when by our vigil we honor in memory the Lord's resurrection which we know for a fact and truthfully acknowledge has only taken place once. Therefore, may God forbid neglect of this solemnity should make irreligious those whom the preaching of the truth has made learned.[4]

The relationship between Christ's Passover and the Church's Passover is regarded here as the relationship between event and sacrament, between history and liturgy of history, between the *semel* and the *quotannis*. The verbs Augustine uses are very exact: he says that the sacrament, or the liturgy, *iterat, renovat* the

56

event. However, he explains very precisely the sense of this "repetition," of this "renewal." It is not meant in a sense that destroys the uniqueness and hence the historicity of the salvific events, thus reducing them to the category of cyclic or recurrent events typical of Greek thought.[5] For it is a question of repetition taking place on another plane: not the plane of history but the plane of liturgy, not of occurrence but of celebration. Liturgy "celebrates" history, "celebrates" having a very strong sense and being equivalent to "keeps alive," "brings to life," "makes present." In other words, the liturgical memorial is both memorial and presence. Through it, the event becomes contemporaneous for us, and we for the event.

When the liturgy is celebrated at this level of awareness and faith, it engages and sways the mind towards the event. It makes us exclaim as the Jews actually used to exclaim at the Passover supper: "We were there, that night! We too passed, not only our forefathers!"[6] "I was crucified with Christ," exclaims St. Gregory Nazianzen in one of his paschal orations, "today I am glorified with him. Yesterday I died with him, today I am revived with him. Yesterday I was buried with him, today I am resurrected with him.'"[7] So the sacrament too becomes an event, but a spiritual, not an historical one. I remember the first Easter celebrated in its revised form in the 1950s. That indeed was a spiritual event for me; I seemed to be celebrating Easter for the first time in my life; at last I was "seized" by the liturgy. When the Sunday of resurrection dawned, I felt as though I, like Jesus, had passed through the Friday of passion and the waiting in the tomb of Holy Saturday. Everything seemed more luminous, even the sound of the bells.

Not everything however was resolved by the distinction between event and sacrament. If, as all ancient tradition affirms, the Church's Passover consists essentially in the Eucharist, the question arises: what is the relationship between the Eucharist celebrated every Sunday and the Passover celebrated only once a year? This was a new problem, peculiar to Christianity. The Jewish liturgy only contained an annual memorial of the Passover, not a weekly one. In some sectors of Christendom—especially among the Greeks—the desire to make as great a distinction as possible between the Christian and the Jewish Passovers (also on account of divergences between Jews and Christians in calculating the correct date for it) led to so great an emphasis on the weekly and daily Passover as to weaken the importance of the annual festival. "Our Passover is celebrated three times each week, sometimes four times, or indeed as often as we wish. For the Passover is not a fast but the offering and sacrifice which is celebrated at each religious service. . . . So, as often as you approach with a clean conscience, you celebrate the Passover."[8]

This, however, was an excessive solution that, taken literally, no longer safeguarded the significance of the annual feast of Easter and destroyed the very idea of "feast day," understood as a united, choral celebration by the whole Church of the saving event, in an atmosphere of special joy. A more balanced solution is that of Augustine: "We ought not to consider these days of Easter so out of the ordinary as to neglect the memorial of the passion and resurrection which we make when we feed on his body and blood day by day. The present feast day, however, has the power of recalling to mind with greater clarity, of exciting greater fervor and of making us rejoice more heartily, inasmuch as, coming around once a year, for us it represents, visually so to speak, the memory of the event."[9] Having so nicely clarified the relationship between the *semel* and the *quotannis* (that is to say between history and liturgy), Augustine in this way also clarifies the relationship between *quotannis* and *quotiescumque,* that is to say between the annual and the daily Passover. Christ's Passover is prolonged in the Church with three rhythms of differing frequency: an annual rhythm which is the feast of Easter; a weekly rhythm which is Sunday; and a daily rhythm which consists in the daily celebration of the Eucharist.

The annual feast is distinct from the simple daily or weekly Eucharist *ratione solemnitatis,* on account of the Solemnity. For that which is celebrated once a year with the recurrence of the event commemorated throws the relationship existing between the sacrament and the event into sharper relief by thus heightening the significance of the liturgical action itself and, by breaking the monotony of the daily rhythm, makes a stronger impression on our faculties. This clarification became part of the patrimony common to the Eastern and Western Church: both regard Sunday as the "little Easter" and the annual festival as the "great Easter."

The relationship between liturgy and grace. The relationship between liturgy and grace is another way of formulating the relationship between liturgy and history. For the grace we are speaking of is not an out-of-time and unhistorical grace, but is literally "the grace of our Lord Jesus Christ," the salvation historically wrought by Jesus in his death and resurrection. The two problems however correspond to two different points of view, two differing sensibilities, so that, while the Latins lay more stress on what we might call the horizontal relationship linking liturgy to history and sacrament to event, the Eastern Fathers, especially Pseudo-Dionysius, being more influenced by Platonism, give greater weight to the as it were vertical perspective linking sacrament to grace, the liturgical rite to the life of the world to come.

In the first case, the liturgy is primarily memorial; in the second, primarily mystery. To investigate the relationship between liturgy and grace therefore entails investigating the mysterial content of the Passover. Here we cannot but admire the wealth of the great mystagogic tradition in the Eastern Church, represented by St. Cyril of Jerusalem, St. Gregory Nazianzen, St. Maximus the Confessor, etc. A magnificent synthesis of their teaching is to be found in a later work: *Life in Christ,* by Nicholas Cabasilas. What Cabasilas has to say about the "mysteries," namely baptism, confirmation, and Eucharist, when taken all together, applies to Easter in which all these sacraments of initiation are reunited.

He sets out from the very simple yet decisive presupposition that "eternal life" (or "new life" or "life in Christ") does not pertain only to the future, but also to the present, in the sense in which St. Thomas too says that grace is the beginning of glory.[10] Hence, Cabasilas affirms, the "mysteries" are the springs or the gates through which this "eternal life" breaks through, in time present, into the Church; they are like windows through which "the Sun of Righteousness enters this dark world, putting life-according-to-the-world to death and causing supernatural life to spring up instead."[11] All this happens by virtue of the principle encapsulated by tradition in the well-known formula: "they cause by signifying." What Cabasilas actually says is: "While we with symbols, as it were *figuratively*, represent the real death that Christ endured for our life, he *in reality* renews us, re-creates us and makes us sharers in his life. Thus, by representing his burial and proclaiming his death in the sacred mysteries, by virtue of these we are begotten, molded and divinely conjoined to the Savior."[12]

In that mysterious leap from symbols to reality lies the mysterial, supernatural, and unconditional character of the sacramental action. Of itself, the liturgical celebration does no more than present signs or symbols of what was performed really and once and for all in Christ. And yet what ensues from it transcends the order of symbols and pertains to reality. "What we have been performing," writes St. Cyril of Jerusalem, "is a likeness (*homoioma*) of death and suffering; whereas of salvation there was no likeness, but the reality."[13]

This mysterial conception of the liturgy stresses God's work to the full. Christ is the true protagonist of salvation, the fighter in the arena. We are like spectators, his fans, cheering and honoring the victor and so deserving the same victor's crown. "Our own contribution consists only in accepting grace, in not wasting the treasure, in not extinguishing the lamp once lit, that is to say in not introducing anything that may be counter to life, anything that can produce death."[14] In fact, however, in this "contribution" there is room for the entire moral commitment of the Christian, and hence one entire section of Cabasilas' work is devoted to the practice of the evangelical beatitudes, treated as the conditions for "safeguarding the life of Christ received from the mysteries."

3. *How to encounter the Lord in the Easter liturgy*

I have traced a somewhat ample picture of the development of paschal liturgy and paschal theology, but I do not wish to stop at this. The Fathers not only elaborated a theology but also a spirituality of the paschal liturgy. They bequeathed us models of liturgical celebrations which are vibrant with faith and fervor. And these can help us put new life into our own celebrations and make them into a true meeting of the community with the Risen Lord.

Now, the question is this: how are we to make a liturgy, and especially the Easter liturgy, into an encounter with the Lord who died and rose again for us, alive today in the Church with his Spirit? From the writings of the Fathers a remarkable spiritual experience emerges: the *cultic epiphany of Christ,* so strong and lively a manifestation of Christ during public worship, especially during the Easter vigil, as to make the faithful say when the service is over, what the disciples said after the resurrection: "We have seen the Lord!" (John 20:25).

In a famous paschal homily of the second century, the bishop at one point stops speaking in his own name and lends his voice to the Risen Lord, who then addresses the congregation in the first person, as he did in the Upper Room on the eve of the Passover:

> "I am the one," says the Christ,
> "I am the one that destroyed death
> and triumphed over the enemy.
> Come then, all you families of peoples
> who are sunk in sins:
> receive the forgiveness of sins.
> For I myself am your forgiveness,
> I am the saving Paschal Victim."[15]

We can understand how St. Ambrose was able to say: "You have shown yourself to me, O Christ, face to face. I have met you in your sacraments."[16] Examples of the same type can be multiplied. The Easter *Exsultet,* whose central point is that cry of joy beginning with the words, "O felix culpa!" gives us an idea of what those ancient paschal celebrations must have been like, and what enthusiasm and hope they were capable of generating among the faithful. If at the mere sound of the *Exsultet* as it rings out at the Easter vigil today, we feel a supernatural shudder run through us, we can imagine what it must have been like when it rang out for the first time in a congregation gathered around its own bishop. One of St. Augustine's sermons, delivered during a paschal vigil, comes to mind. From it one gets the impression that, to some degree, bishop and people enjoy a foretaste of the Passover in the heavenly Jerusalem: "What joy, dear friends! Joy in all being gathered together here; joy in singing the psalms and hymns; joy in remembering Christ's passion and resurrection; joy in our hope of the life to come! If hope alone gives such happiness, what will possession do? In these days, as we hear the Alleluia ring out, our spirits are as though transfigured. Do we not seem to taste something of that supernal city?"[17] One can understand why those faithful who were lucky enough to have such pastors and such liturgies waited with holy impatience for the coming of the paschal vigil, "mother of all holy vigils," and kept saying to one another these words that have come down to us: "When will the vigil be? How many days now until the vigil?"[18]

What was the secret of this extraordinary power of the rites? I think one reason was, without question, the faith and holiness of the pastors. But there were failures among them even then, and not all the bishops were saints or poets. What else? A much greater role was accorded to the action of the Holy Spirit as light of the rites and soul of the liturgy. Of Melito of Sardis, whom I have already mentioned, we read that in all things "he acted in the Holy Spirit"[19] St. Basil says that the Holy Spirit is the "place of doxology," that is to say the ideal place, or the temple, from which alone it is possible to contemplate God and adore him "in Spirit and in truth"; he is "the choirmaster" of those who sing God's praises; he it is who "fortifies" the Church during the rite, so that she can stand worthily before her Lord.[20]

The Risen Jesus "was brought to life in the Spirit" (1 Pet 3:18); only the Holy Spirit can make him present and make it so that he manifests himself behind the rites and words. Only the Holy Spirit can make the veil fall from our eyes and hearts and let us recognize Jesus when he is spoken of and his bread is broken. As we leave the liturgical assembly, he it is who prompts us to turn to our friends, like the disciples at Emmaus, and say: Jesus is alive! We recognized him in the breaking of the bread!

What is there to prevent the Holy Spirit today too from being the conductor of the rites, on whom the eyes of all are fixed, rather than on the outward conductor of the ceremony? What is there to prevent us from hoping for a renewal in today's Church of that miracle of the liturgy which would allow us to meet the Risen Christ alive with his Spirit in the Church? In the days of the Fathers, the action of the Spirit in the unfolding of the rites was certainly made easier by the fact that not everything was fixed in advance; there was room for the inspiration of the moment, for the originality and unpredictability of the Spirit, especially when the bishop was presiding at the liturgy.

But the essential conditions for that miracle are always present in the Church. And they are better today than they were in the past, now that the liturgical reform has brought the paschal rites back to the splendor and simplicity of their primitive form and to the language of the people. (For the Fathers didn't use Greek or Latin because it was the universal language of the day but because it was their language, the people's language.) All we need to do is put the ever new wine of faith and the Holy Spirit into these "new wineskins," the renovated Easter ceremonies. The priest who presides over the liturgy can be of great help to the congregation in this. Looking at him, the faithful should be able to see his face become radiant while, like Moses, he converses with God (cf. Exod 34:29).

May the Lord grant that we too, as we come out from the Easter ceremonies, may be able to exclaim, as the first disciples did to Thomas, who had not been there: "We have seen the Lord!"

NOTES

1. St. Augustine, *Enarrationes in Psalmos* 120.6 (CCL 40, p. 1791).
2. *Paschal homily* of antique authorship (SCh 36, p. 61).
3. Chromatius of Aquileia, *Sermon 16 for the Great Night* (SCh 154, p. 259).
4. St. Augustine, *Sermo* 220 (PL 38, 1089).
5. Against such an eventuality's occurring, see St. Augustine, *City of God* 12.13, 17, 20; and St. Gregory Nazianzen, *Epistola* 101 (PG 37, 192).
6. *Pesachim* 10.5.
7. St. Gregory Nazianzen, *Oratio in Sanctum Pascha* 1.4 (PG 36, 397).
8. St. John Chrysostom, *Adversus Iudaeos homilia*, 3.4 (PG 48, 867).
9. St. Augustine, *Sermo Wilmart* 9.2 (PLS 2, 725).
10. St. Thomas Aquinas, *Summa theologiae* 2-2.24.3.2.
11. Nicholas Cabasilas, *Vita in Christo* 1.3 (PG 150, 504).
12. Ibid. (PG 150, 501).
13. St. Cyril of Jerusalem, *Catechesis mystagogica* 2.7 (PG 33, 1084).
14. Nicholas Cabasilas, *Vita in Christo* 1.2 (PG 150, 501).
15. Melito of Sardis, *On Pascha* 102–3 (SCh 123, p. 122).
16. St. Ambrose, *Apologia Prophetae David* 58 (PL 14, 875).
17. St. Augustine, *Sermo Morin-Guelferbytanus* 8.2 (PLS 2, 557).
18. Cf. St. Augustine, *Sermon* 219 (PL 38, 1088); and *Sermo Guelferbytanus* 5.2. (SCh 116, 213).
19. Eusebius, *Historia ecclesiastica* 5.24.5.
20. Cf. St. Basil, *De Spiritu Sancto* 26 (PG 32, 181); and *Anafora* of St. Basil.

Chapter Five

"O Happy Fault!"

The Paschal Mystery in the Liturgy (2)

1. *Easter and mystagogic catechesis*

In the early centuries of the Church the most advanced kind of religious instruction was known as "mystagogic catechesis," an introduction to the mysteries. Usually this took place after, not before, baptism and was conducted by the bishop in person.

St. Ambrose explains the two fundamental reasons for this type of catechesis. The first is pedagogic: that which is revealed all at once, having been waited for for a long time, makes a deeper impression and stays in the mind longer than what is revealed little by little over a more extended period of time. The second is prudential: to reveal the holiest mysteries to someone not yet fully a member of the Church would mean exposing these mysteries to the danger of profanation. "Now," Ambrose writes, "the time invites us to speak about the mysteries and to set forth the very purpose of the sacraments. If we had thought that this should have been taught to those not yet initiated before baptism, we should be considered to have betrayed, rather than to have portrayed, the mysteries; then there is the consideration that the light of the mysteries will infuse itself better in the unsuspecting than if some sermon had preceded them."[1]

The particular point about this catechesis, which accounts for its undying fascination, is the fact that it synthesized truth and experience, abstract knowledge and concrete perception. During their preparation for baptism, the catechumens had learned the truths of religion and been taught about the events of salvation history; then, with baptism, they had completed the rites of initiation. Now, for the first time, the flashover, so to speak, occurred between knowledge and experience. The nexus between the historical events performed by Christ and the liturgical rites was unveiled.

In the initiation rites, the reality had been conveyed by symbolism and this kindled faith and enthusiasm. St. Augustine explains the phenomenon thus:

> Anything that is suggested by means of symbols strikes and kindles our affection much more forcefully than the truth itself would do if presented unadorned with mysterious symbols. . . . Our sensibility is less easily kindled when still involved in purely concrete realities, but if it is first turned towards symbols drawn from the corporeal world, and thence again to the plane of those spiritual realities signified by those symbols, it gathers strength by the mere act of passing from one to the other and, like the flame of a burning torch, is made by the motion to burn all the brighter.[2]

Something of the same sort took place in mystagogic catechesis. The truths of religion—universal and remote—were perceived in a concrete, personal way, owing to the still vivid memory of water on the body, oil on the head, and the white garment that the candidates wore. The liveliest faith is that which blossoms from seeing and hearing at once. St. Cyril of Jerusalem made a great point of this. "It has long been my wish," he said to his neophytes, "to discourse to you on these spiritual, heavenly mysteries. On the principle, however, that seeing is believing, I delayed until the present occasion, calculating that, after what you saw that night, I should find you a readier audience when I am to be your guide to the brighter and more fragrant meadows of this second Eden."[3]

The specific feature distinguishing mystagogic catechesis is not therefore the fact of putting figures and realities (i.e., the types of the Old Testament and the Christian realities) into relationship with one another. This constitutes the typological element common to all patristic catechesis. One has only to compare the pre-baptismal catecheses attributed to the same St. Cyril with his five mystagogic catecheses to see that typological explanation plays an even more prominent part in the former than in the latter. The particular point about mystagogic catechesis consists in another relationship which includes the preceding as a part of it. This is the relationship established between the *events* of salvation history, first prefigured, then fulfilled (i.e., figures and reality together), and the *rites* which in present time make operant and renew these same events. In other words, mystagogic catechesis consists in the explanation of the rite performed, where "explanation" does not mean some personal, allegorical, or edifying interpretation but the effective nexus between a given rite and an event. It is the principle expressed in Latin sacramental theology by the famous maxim, *Significando causant*: "while signifying, they produce," or "they produce what they signify." Therefore, by reproducing in imagery the death and resurrection of Christ, we do not attain merely the *image* of salvation, but the *reality*.

The schema according to which mystagogic catechesis was unfolded to the neophyte was a simple one. The bishop referred one by one to the rites received; then he put the question: "What is the meaning of this rite?" "Last Saturday we performed the rite of 'the opening,' when the bishop touched your ears and nostrils. What does this mean?"[4] And then follows the explanation or the unveiling of the mystery contained in this rite and its relationship to Jesus' act when he shouted to the deaf mute: "*Effetha,* Be opened!*"

Jewish Passover mystagogy

Now it is important to note that this schema originated with the Passover. "When your children ask you," we read in the Book of Exodus, " 'What does this rite of yours mean?' you shall reply, 'This is the Passover sacrifice of the LORD, who passed over the houses of the Israelites in Egypt; when he struck down the Egyptians, he spared our houses" (Exod 12:26-27). Here we have the explanation of certain rites and signs in relation to past events, made in the framework of an initiation or of a commemoration liturgy, we have a mystagogic catechesis. The reference to the event in this case consists in commemorating God's saving act at the time of the Exodus from Egypt.

The history of the Jewish Passover exhibits a remarkable feature, as we have already noted. In late Judaism and particularly in New Testament times, there existed two quite different ways of interpreting and celebrating the Passover; one way, peculiar to Palestinian Judaism, influenced by the Temple and the priesthood, and another way, peculiar to the Judaism of the Diaspora, which we know about mainly through Philo of Alexandria. In the former, the mystagogic character of the Passover celebration was preserved, thanks to the presence of a Passover liturgy, a priesthood, and a Temple; in the second, this character disap-

peared. In parallel we see that while the Palestinian liturgical Passover retains a strongly salvation-historical character (the protagonist is God, who passes and saves, and the rite makes the event operant), the Hellenistic Passover of the Diaspora assumes a predominantly moral character, the protagonist is human nature, and the Passover consists in passing from vice to virtue, from the physical to the spiritual.

Two texts will be sufficient to illustrate these two concepts of the Passover in Judaism. The first reflects the liturgical Passover of Palestinian Judaism which Jesus celebrated with his apostles during his lifetime, even though the fixing of its form dates to after A.D. 70.

> Rabbi Gamaliel used to affirm: He who at Passover has not uttered these three words has not fulfilled his obligation. They are *Pessah* (Passover), *Matzah* (Unleavened Bread) and *Maror* (Bitter Herbs). *Pessah* which our forefathers ate when the Temple existed—why? This is why: Because God 'passed over' the houses of our forefathers. . . . *Matsah*, this unleavened bread, why do we eat it? This is why: because our forefathers had no time to ferment the dough. . . . *Maror,* these bitter herbs, why do we eat them? This is why: because the Egyptians embittered the lives of our forefathers in Egypt.''[5]

By key words, as we see, the principal Passover rites are evoked, and for each an explanation is given, introduced by the appropriate question: "Why do we do this?" The mysterial realism, by which that which is signified is brought about, is expressed in the concluding words of the text: "In every generation, everyone should think of himself as though he had personally come out of Egypt."

And here, by way of contrast, is a passage from Philo, reflecting the other, moral concept of the Passover: "For those who are used to turning things narrated (history!) into allegory, the feast of Passover signifies the purification of the soul. For they affirm that whoever loves wisdom is interested in nothing but passing from the body and the passions to the virtues."[6] The Passover is seen here too as symbolizing something else, but here we have a symbolism very different from that of liturgy and ritual. Here it is not the paschal rite, the supper, which is the sign of the historical event, that is to say, of God's passing and of the

Exodus from Egypt, but the historical event itself which is symbolic of an eternal idea and of a spiritual fact. The protagonist of this Passover, the one who does the passing, is not God but human nature. To the mysterial fact succeeds the ethical.

CHRISTIAN PASSOVER MYSTAGOGY

Let us pass on now to the Christian Passover. Starting from the second century, we observe the same polarity in it between a mysterial and an ethical Passover. There are areas and authors where a mystagogic catechesis of Easter prevails and areas and authors where the other type of catechesis prevails, i.e., the moral and spiritual. Of mystagogic stamp are the most ancient paschal homilies that have come down to us, especially those of Quartodeciman origin. Of moral and spiritual stamp is the paschal catechesis of Origen or that influenced by him.[7] What one may call the horizontal relationship of mystagogic catechesis (rites—salvation-history events) is abolished or declared to be secondary with respect to what one may term the vertical relationship: historical events and sacramental rites on the one hand, intelligible realities on the other.

This second and moral type of catechesis has its incontrovertible merits too and often touches peaks of true mysticism, but it is not the same thing as mysterial catechesis. It lays more stress on human effort than on the gratuitous and prevenient initiative of God in Christ which we are to make our own by faith and the sacraments. It is designed to "introduce to the mysteries," but here mysteries (*sacramenta*) have a different sense. It is not so much the mystery linked to salvation-history and sacramental rites as the "deep meanings" or "the mysteries of the world to come" which are attained by going beyond the letter.[8]

This preamble about paschal mystagogy had a practical and pastoral aim: to show how the paschal liturgy and in particular the vigil, understood and lived to the full, still constitutes even today the great mystagogic catechesis of the year, the unique opportunity for inducting the faithful into the inexhaustible depths of the Christian mystery.

A patristic text which anticipates the ringing tones of the *Exsultet* calls Easter eve "the Church's nymphagogue," that is to say, she who conducts the bride to the bridegroom's house and puts her in possession of her heritage:

O night, desire of the year,
O night, nymphagogue of the Church,
O night, mother of neophytes,
O night in which the heir
    inducts the heiress into the inheritance!'"[9]

In order to discover this new catechetical and mystagogic dimension of Easter, let us turn our attention forthwith to the texts of the paschal vigil and first of all to the paschal proclamation, the *Exsultet*, "this peerless masterpiece of the Christian lyric genius, which for the faithful represents the discovery of the Easter mystery, the proclamation of Christ's universal triumph and the absoluteness of redemption" (B. Capelle). It is indeed a mystagogic catechesis about Easter, in the lyric key. For it sets out from the concrete rites and signs—the night, the vigil, the lighting of the candle—revealing their profound significance by the light of the figures of the Old Testament and the realities of the New.

Let us try to gather the very rich theological content of the text around two main points: first, Easter as the fulfillment of all salvation history; second, Easter as the renewal of the world. In antiquity, during the week following Easter, the neophytes, full of joyful anticipation, came back to church in white garments to receive their initiation into the great mysteries of faith from the bishop in person. Most Christians today, having been baptized in very different circumstances, have never received their mystagogic catechesis. If we care to, this is an opportunity for making good this deficiency. Let ours be a neophyte's heart once more: let us return, not a week but perhaps years and tens of years after our baptism, to the feet of Mother Church, with new eyes to contemplate the splendor of the mysteries of our faith. Like newborn babes too, let us long for pure spiritual milk, so that through it we may grow into salvation (cf. 1 Pet 2:2).

2. *"This is the night": Easter, the fulfillment of salvation history*

This is the paschal feast wherein is slain the true Lamb whose blood hallows the door-posts of the faithful. This is the night on which you caused our forefathers, the sons of Israel, in their passage out of Egypt, to pass dry-shod over the Red Sea. This is the night which purged away the blackness of sin by the light of the fiery pillar. This is the night which at this hour throughout the world restores to grace and yokes to holiness those who believe in Christ, detaching them from worldly vice and all the murk of sin. On this night Christ burst the bonds of death and rose victorious from the grave.''[10]

THE SPIRITUAL INTERPRETATION OF THE BIBLE

These words, like everything else in the Christian paschal liturgy, plunge us headlong into the spiritual interpretation of the Bible. They make us see immediately what it consists in, not by explaining it but by practicing it. Saying "This is the night when the Israelites crossed the Red Sea,'' is the same as saying that that event tended to this one, that that Passover was orientated to this one, that in Christ's Passover it received its full significance and revealed all the promises with which it was charged.

Christian tradition recognizes, as Henri de Lubac made so clear, two senses of Scripture: a literal sense and a spiritual sense. These two senses are to each other as the Old Testament and the New Testament. Their relationship is, however, of a quite particular type. The second emerges from the first, without annulling it. It does not destroy it but, to the contrary, by completing it, brings it to life and renews it. It transfigures it and subsumes it. We are not talking of some slow evolution but of a sudden change, as a result of which everything takes on a new meaning. It is the critical moment of transition from the temporal to the eternal.

All this occurs in Christ's sacrificial act, in the "hour" of the cross, when, referring not only to his own life but to all the Scriptures, Jesus cries out: "*Consummatum est,* it is finished!" (John 19:30). The cross is the universal interpretative key, the moment when the lamb opens the "scroll sealed with seven seals" (cf. Rev 5:1f.), which is the Old Testament. It is the boundary uniting—and at the same time distinguishing—the two Testaments and the two Covenants. "Clear and glowing, behold now the great page that separates the two Testaments! All doors fly open, all conflicts are dispelled, all contradictions are resolved" (P. Claudel).[11]

If we compare the totality of salvation history to the unfolding of a Mass, Christ's Passover represents the moment of the consecration, when the signs—the bread and wine—are transformed into Christ's body and blood. As the species of bread and wine are not depreciated and debased by the fact of becoming Christ's body and blood but are raised by this to highest dignity,

70

so are the figures of the Old Testament, by virtue of being replaced by reality, by Christ. A very ancient paschal author expresses this sudden transformation thus:

> The slaying of the sheep
> and the sacrifice of the lamb
> and the scripture of the law
> have found fulfilment in Jesus Christ,
> on whose account were all things in the ancient law. . . .
> Now the law has become Word
> and the old, new . . .
> and the commandment, grace
> and the figure, reality
> and the lamb, the Son.''[12]

Sometimes the Fathers of the Church get carried away too far in this direction, as when the very author just quoted compares the ancient Passover to a wax, or clay, or wooden model which is destroyed once the work of art or building has been made, for the preparation of which it had been used.[13] This is not the correct Christian typological sense and, what is more, Melito himself and the other Fathers were far from ''throwing out'' the Old Testament, which they were indeed constantly putting to good use. Present-day dialogue with the Jewish world has taught us to be more attentive and respectful towards the perennial values which the Old Testament conserves for the Jews, quite apart from the way Christians interpret it[14].

True, the ''letter kills'' (2 Cor 3:6), and to go on seeing in the events of the Old Testament only what they originally signified, and without reference to Christ, would be infidelity to Scripture itself, just as if we were to go on seeing only bread and wine on the altar after the consecration. But whom does the letter kill? The Jews, the devotees of the Old Covenant who, following the faith of their ancestors in all good conscience, cling to the traditions handed down and in this spirit celebrate the old Passover year after year? No, it kills the Christians! Those Christians who, having by grace known Christ and believed in him who is ''the fulfillment of the law,'' go on only seeing in the Old Testament the letter, thus reducing it to a book which is only of interest for studying the development of Jewish history and religion.

The typological or spiritual interpretation of the Fathers and of Tradition is not what endangers the lasting value of the Old

Testament; this danger comes rather from historico-critical exegesis when it is shut in on itself, denying the Old Testament any prophetic quality and any opening to the supernatural and to Christ. This new method of exegesis, originating in the Enlightenment, reached its apogee in the last century with actual denigration of the Old Testament, to the point where it was affirmed that the difference between the Jewish and Christian consciousness, between the Jewish and Christian Scriptures, was as profound as that existing between paganism and Christianity (F. Schleiermacher). In the wake of Hegel, for whom Christianity was religion in its absolute form, the Jewish religion, like paganism, became no more than a necessary, transitory moment in the evolution towards the absolute. Being transitory, the Old Testament was useful in its own period only; once that stage is over, it is seen to be empty. This evolutionary or "dialectical" surpassing of the Old Testament is quite another thing from that intended by the spiritual or typological interpretation. The latter, far from devaluing the Old Testament, exalts it to the highest. The Christian Passover, far from debasing the Jewish Passover, enhances it: not only the Passover codified in the Bible but also the one still lived and celebrated by the Jewish people year after year.

Let us now give rather closer consideration to what the *Exsultet* puts at the center of that decisive act which marks the transition from figure to reality, to what precisely it makes Christ's Passover consist in. This is a good opportunity for us to verify how much, of all that rich debate on the meaning of the word *Passover* which took place in the early Christian centuries (which we recalled to mind in our first chapter), has actually entered the liturgy.

The Passover, says the *Exsultet*, is the feast "wherein is slain the true Lamb" (and this will be repeated in the Preface for Easter Day). Here we are in line with 1 Corinthians 5:7: "For our paschal lamb, Christ, has been sacrificed," and hence in line with the ancient interpretation of Passover as *passion*. But Passover is also the time when "Christ burst the bonds of death and rose victorious from the grave." So it is also the feast of the *resurrection*. Besides this *historical* and Christological dimension of Passover,

72

a gesture is however also made towards the tradition which explains the Passover as a *moral* passing of human nature "from vice to virtue and from sin to grace." For the Passover, it says, tears human nature "away from the vices of this world and from the darkness of sin, by restoring it to grace."

But let us restrict the field of vision even further. What is it in all these things that constitutes the real fulcrum of salvation? What is it that gives Christ's Passover that absolute and universal significance which makes it sufficient to save the whole human race for all time? The answer lies in the words *redeem, redemption, Redeemer,* which take us right to the theological core of the *Exsultet.* "Without redemption," it says, "life itself would have been no boon." Jesus himself is described as "the great and mighty Redeemer: *talis ac tantus redemptor.*"[15]

We all know that it is characteristic of Latin theology to conceive of salvation—following St. Paul—as redemption from sin, made possible by the sacrificial death of Christ. St. Augustine said in one of his Easter sermons: "We were in debt; we were in debt to just such an extent as we had sinned. He came without debt because he was without sin; he found us oppressed by a deadly and accursed debt and, paying what he had not stolen (cf. Ps 69:5), he mercifully freed us from everlasting debt. We had acknowledged our guilt and we were expecting punishment, but he, having become not an accomplice in our fault but a sharer in our penalty, wished to cancel both fault and punishment."[16] St. Anselm, and St. Thomas after him, were to take up this inheritance and give it a formulation destined to become classic, with the theory of vicarious satisfaction. Sin violated God's rights. Atonement is required in order to make reparation for the offense and re-establish God's rights. But, since the gravity of an offense is not measured by the person of the offender but by that of the person offended, who in this case was God himself, obviously reparation was needed on a scale infinitely beyond what any human being could offer.[17] Such, therefore, was the situation, allowing no way out, before the coming of Christ: on the one hand, humanity had to pay the debt but could not do so; on the other, God who could pay but should not do so, not having committed the fault. In an unforeseeable manner the incarnation resolved this state of affairs. For in Christ, who is both human and divine, are found united, in the same person, he who *ought to* pay the debt and he who alone *can* do it.

73

All this is marvelously put in the *Exsultet*, where it says: "He repaid Adam's debt for us to his eternal Father, and with his dear blood wiped out the penalty of that ancient sin."[18] This is a view of salvation derived straight from the New Testament. There we read that Christ came to give his life "as a ransom for many" (Matt 20:28); in his blood we have "redemption and the forgiveness of transgressions" (Eph 1:7; 1 Cor 1:30; 1 Tim 2:6); God has made him serve as an "instrument of expiation" (Rom 3:25); on the cross Christ has cancelled "the bond against us, with its legal claims" (Col 2:14).

The theological view extracted from these texts has sometimes been weighed down and obscured by excesses, as in the case of the theory according to which the ransom was paid by Christ to the devil, to whom the human race, by sinning, had sold itself into slavery. In our liturgical text, there is nothing remotely like this. Christ has paid the debt on our behalf "to the eternal Father."

Even so, however, the explanation is open to a disquieting objection. Famous preachers in the past let themselves go overboard in their Good Friday sermons, when speaking of "the anger of an incensed God"; "Jesus prays," says Bossuet, "and the enraged Father will not listen to him; this is the justice of a God avenging the affronts he has received; Jesus suffers and the Father is not appeased."[19] And a God like this can still be called "Father"?

In the *Exsultet*, this danger is eliminated at the root because the juridical point of view is supplemented and immediately corrected by another which frees it from any negative connotation of cold justice, bringing it back to the revelation of God as love. True, the Son has paid the debt to the eternal Father; but the Father not only receives the ransom price, he also pays it. He indeed pays the highest price of all, since he has given his only Son: "How wonderful the condescension of your mercy towards us," exclaims the *Exsultet*, addressing the Father, "How far beyond all reckoning your loving-kindness; to ransom your slave, you gave up your Son!"[20] Rarely has Christian thought in any of its manifestations reached such depth of insight! Rarely has God the Father's invincible love for the human race been hymned with greater conviction or simplicity. There is an echo here of Romans 8:32: "God did not spare his own Son, but handed him over for us all!"

3. "O happy fault!": Easter as renewal of the world

So far I have dealt with the perspective which presents the Passover as the fulfillment of all salvation history by means of Christ's redemptive act on the cross. Another, more positive perspective, however, is intertwined with this in the paschal liturgy and even in the *Exsultet*: that of the Passover as the renewal of the world (*renovatio mundi*) and as cosmic palingenesis. First let us see, briefly, how this tradition came to be formed, and then how it found its way into the liturgy of the Church.

"Why is the month of the Passover called the first month of the year?" (cf. Exod 12:2). To this question, a Christian author of the end of the second or the beginning of the third century replies: "The explanation secretly current among the Jews has it that this was when God the designer and creator of all things created the universe."[21] This information is correct. In the Jewish paschal catechesis, the "secret" idea—i.e., one not contained in the canonical books—was affirmed that the world had had its beginning at the spring equinox and that therefore the Passover was the anniversary of the creation: the birthday, we might say. "In the spring equinox," writes Philo, "we have a replica and a reflection of that first one in which this world was made. Thus, year by year, God reminds us about the creation of the world."[22] A Jewish paschal text, possibly pre-dating the New Testament, sums up all sacred history in "four nights": the night of creation, the night of the sacrifice of Isaac, the night of the Exodus from Egypt, and the last night when the world will be dissolved.[23] All these nights meet in the Passover, insofar as they all occurred or will occur at the same time of the year, on the night of the Passover.

This tradition passed very early into Christian catechesis, favored by the fact that the Apostle too had spoken of Christ's Passover and of baptism as of a new creation (cf. 2 Cor 5:17; Gal 6:15). "This," exclaims St. Cyril of Jerusalem, "is the season of the creation of the world. At that very season when occurred the loss of the image of God, occurred its restitution."[24] The forms which this theme assumes in Christian paschal catechesis are countless. Possibly its most elaborate expression is to be found in a homily written for Easter A.D. 387. In it the Passover is described as "recapitulation," "re-creation," "renewal," "restoration," "rectification": all words that indicate a reversal of the course of the world by bringing it back to its beginnings.

Wanting to procure the resurrection for fallen human nature, wanting to renew it and re-create it by means of his passion in its original state, behold what the only-begotten Son of God did! Himself the creator of the first man, he also wanted to be his savior after he had fallen, with a view to restoring all nature. Not content therefore with consigning himself to the passion, to effect this renewal he re-united all those chronological elements which had existed in the creation, so that the end might seem in harmony with the beginning and the creator's way of acting consistent in itself."[25]

This author's most original idea is that of the renewal, not only of the reality of the world and human nature, but also of time. God created "a very pure time"; sin, however, polluted time, since committed in time. And now, at Easter, God renews that "very pure time," since Christ's death and resurrection take place "in time." To show that original time has been restored, God causes all those temporal circumstances (equinox, full moon, and sixth day of the week) which had coincided at the moment when Adam was created, once again to be united at Christ's death.[26]

This grandiose vision soon found its way into the liturgy; for there the Church has always collected, by a process, as it were, of sieving, purifying, and reducing to essentials, the best of what is discovered in the Word of God, owing to theological development and contact with new cultures. The choice of Genesis 1, the story of the creation, as the first reading at the paschal vigil is connected with this tradition and is intended to convey that Easter is a new creation. A wonderful prayer, dating back to the seventh-century Gelasian Sacramentary and happily re-introduced at the recent liturgical reform into the vigil texts—after the seventh reading, to be precise—says "May the world see the fallen lifted up, the old made new, and all things brought to perfection, through him who is their origin, our Lord Jesus Christ."

So too the *Exsultet* echoes the theme of Easter as cosmic renewal. "Let earth," it says, "be joyful in the radiance of this great splendor. Enlightened by the glory of her eternal King, let her feel that from the whole round world the darkness has been lifted."[27] And again: "By this night's holiness crime is banished and sin washed away; innocence is restored to the fallen and gladness to the sorrowful. It drives forth hate, brings peace, and humbles tyranny."[28]

The *Exsultet*, however, carries this vision one step further. Before, the subject was a backward renewal (*renovatio in pristinum*), a bringing things back to what they had been at the beginning; now, however, the subject is a forward-looking renewal, one better than before (*renovatio in melius*). "O truly necessary sin of Adam that Christ's blood blotted out, and happy fault that merited such a Redeemer!"[29] Boldness never again equalled in Christian thought! As a result, people found it somewhat alarming: so much so in some local Churches that these two sentences were omitted from the tenth century onwards; not in Rome however, where the *Exsultet* was never robbed of this theological and lyrical high-spot.

What mind could have conceived the cry, "O felix culpa," "O happy fault"? What authority stands behind it? Not just the authority of an obscure writer (the *Exsultet*, it seems, was composed in Gaul sometime in the fifth century), but that of a doctor of the Church. For this daring theology is inspired, almost literally, by St. Ambrose. He, speaking of Adam's fault, had exclaimed: "Happy the ruin that was amended for the better!",[30] and again: "For me, my fault became the price of redemption. . . . My fault profited me more than innocence."[31] St. Ambrose, however, was in his turn leaning on the even greater authority of Scripture, which assures us that "where sin increased, grace overflowed all the more" (Rom 5:20). Certainly, the "O felix culpa" says something more. It is a cry of hope and optimism, not finding its justification in any scriptural text taken in isolation but rather in the Scriptures as a whole, uttered in the conviction that the power of God is so great that it can use even sin (*etiam peccata*, as St. Augustine said) for his glory and our good.[32]

The cry's extraordinary beauty lies in the enthusiasm it evinces for the person of Christ, "the great and mighty Redeemer!" To a universe without fault and without Christ is openly preferred a universe with fault but with Christ. And who could give the lie to the author who first dared say this? A famous medieval mystic, in the optimistic line of descent from the *Exsultet*, wrote the following words, which she says she heard from God: "Sin is inevitable, but all shall be well, and all shall be well, and all manner of thing shall be well."[33]

4. *"O great and holy Easter!"*: a glance at the Easter of our Oriental brothers

It would not be hard, were it necessary for our purpose, to show how the same themes of the Western paschal liturgy are also to be found, though with a different coloration, in the Oriental and Byzantine liturgy. It too constitutes a magnificent mystagogic catechesis.

I say "with a different coloration," and this is what gives the comparison its value. The two liturgies are really like two lungs, with which the entire body of the Church can breathe the more amply; they are like two eyes which, looking at an object from different angles, can see it in proper perspective. "So great a mystery cannot be reached by one sole route," says an old maxim, referring to God (*uno itinere non potest perveniri ad tam grande secretum*). This is also true for the paschal mystery. Comparison of the two traditions serves not only to expand our horizon and give us a more comprehensive idea of the mystery, but also to give us a better grasp of our own tradition and spirituality.

The central idea of the Latin vision of salvation, as we have said, is that of ransom, of redemption, which, principally inspired by St. Paul, puts the accent on the paschal mystery. The idea central to Greek theology is divinization, which, more closely inspired by St. John, throws the accent on the incarnation. Provoked by Arianism which denied the full divinity of Christ, the Greek Fathers were prompted to advance the divinization of the Christian as result and proof of the divinity of Christ: "Christ divinizes us, therefore he is God," "Christ is God, therefore he divinizes us." Hence the importance of the incarnation, seen as the moment when God descends into the bosom of the human race and, by taking on human nature, sanctifies it and confers incorruptibility upon it.

Now, we know that these two points of view—incarnation and paschal mystery—have never been rightly held as being separate from or alternative to one another. The Greek Fathers look on Easter as the final completion of the incarnation and, in a certain sense, as its purpose: "Christ was born so that he could die," says St. Gregory of Nyssa.[34] The Latin Fathers, for their part, see the incarnation as the presupposition on which Easter is based. Christ's redemption is absolute and universal, since wrought by One who is at once divine and human and who, as God, confers

78

a value transcending time and space on what he does.

Even so, it cannot be denied that there is a difference of accent between the two traditions, and this is also faithfully reflected in their respective paschal liturgies. The dominant theme in the paschal texts of the Byzantine liturgy is not that of redemption from sin but rather of consecration and of bringing everyone new life. At Easter it especially celebrates Christ's triumph over death and hell: the triumph of life. Christ's descent into Hades is the paschal theme *par excellence*, and this is what is represented in the icon of the feast. The ever-repeated explanation is that death and the devil have attacked Christ's mortal flesh but inside have found the Godhead and been destroyed by it. "Thanks to the Spirit who could not die, Christ has slain Death, who slew the human race."[35]

This is how this victorious Easter is hymned at the end of the ancient paschal homily already mentioned; its accents are also to be found in the texts of the Byzantine paschal liturgy:

> O mystic sight! O spiritual feast! O divine Passover! From heaven you come down to earth and from earth again you rise to heaven. O feast-day common to all things! O festival of the whole cosmos! O joy of the universe, its honor, its banquet and delight! By you, grim death was destroyed and life has been diffused on all beings. Heaven's gates have opened; God has appeared as a human being and human beings have risen as God. By you, hell's gates were taken off their hinges and their iron bolts broken. The people in the underworld rose from the dead on receiving the good news, and to the celestial ranks a choir was furnished by the earth. O divine Passover, to us you have spiritually united the God whom the heavens cannot contain. By you, the great wedding-chamber has been filled; all wear the wedding garment, nor is anyone thrown out for not having a wedding garment."[36]

"Passover" here is virtually synonymous with "Christ," in accordance with the ancient equation: "The Passover is Christ."

The theme of Easter as universal renewal and return to paradise also rings out in this new, victorious key, in a passage of the Byzantine Easter liturgy:

> A divine Passover has been revealed today . . .
> A new, holy Passover, a mysterious Passover . . .
> A Passover opening the gates of paradise to us,

A Passover sanctifying all the faithful . . .
This is the day of the Resurrection!
Let us radiate joy for the sake of this feast,
Let us embrace one another,
Call those who hate us brothers too,
Forgive all for the sake of the Resurrection.[37]

I have always thought that one subject alone would have been worthy of the choral music that closes Beethoven's Ninth Symphony: Christ's resurrection. Only this would have constituted an adequate "text" for music so sublime. And lo, now in this liturgical hymn, written so many centuries before, we find virtually the same words as in Schiller's "Ode to Joy," set to music by Beethoven ("Embrace one another, ye millions: this kiss for everyone. All men will be brothers, once brushed by the light wings of joy"). But the joy sung here does not exist, it is only longed for, whereas our Easter hymn speaks of a joy come about and offered to us all. It is based on the objective fact, constantly repeated in the Easter Troparion, that:

Christ has risen from the dead,
by his own death he has destroyed death
and given life to the dead in their graves.

5. How is the Church to hand on the heritage to her children?

There was a time in the history of the Church, in its very early days, when Easter was, so to speak, everything. As yet there were no other feasts in the year to absorb aspects of the content of salvation history, so breaking it up and fatally rupturing its unity. In Easter, all sacred history, from its beginnings to its fulfillment in Christ, and the entire career of Christ himself, from his birth to his second coming, came to life in a potent synthesis. Then the Christian mystery lived its brief phase of unity, before "being scattered over the face of the earth," and before its light became refracted into as many different colors as there are feast-days in the liturgical year or, in another sphere, theological treatises. The liturgy, we have seen, has preserved a pretty faithful memory of that happy period, and the recent reform of the Easter ceremonies has brought back to light in the Latin Church, in so far as it was possible to do so without ignoring history, this original countenance of Easter. Because of this, it constitutes today the most splendid of mystagogic catecheses, the best introduction to the depths of the Christian mystery.

The question we now ought to ask ourselves is this: how are we to put life into this inheritance and transmit it alive and ever new to our own generation? How can we recover the enthusiasm that made a Father of the Church exclaim: "O great and holy Easter, I speak of you as of a living being!"[38] How can we act so that Easter can truly be the awaited time when the Church, as Asterius said above, "is inducted into the inheritance" and in turn inducts her children into it? In the trunk of a tree, each passing year leaves a ring that shows its annual growth. What can we do so that every Easter will leave a similar ring in the lives of Christians and not go by in vain?

We can no longer count on just repeating the ancient formularies (be it even that most beautiful Easter Proclamation, the *Exsultet*) since, having been conceived in another language and culture, they inevitably lose their force, once translated into another language and deprived, into the bargain, of the Gregorian musical accompaniment which made them all the more loved. In any case, frequent repetition, even in the original form, attenuates their emotive charge and their power over the imagination. *Assueta vilescunt!* There is no point in simply regretting the loss of Latin and complaining about its disappearance from our ordinary services. This would be to ignore an elementary observation: that when these texts were written they were in the language spoken by the people, not in another language. Had they reasoned as some who yearn after Latin do today, the *Exsultet* would had to have been written in Greek, not in Latin, Greek having been the liturgical language in Rome and the West for the first two centuries.

So we need a middle way between these venerable texts and ourselves, and this kind of middle way can only come about through the ministry of the word. One way of helping to keep the patrimony of the Easter vigil alive can be the holding of special celebrations where the vigil is celebrated in its integral form, not reduced either in length or in shape, with a preparation and in an atmosphere inspired by those of the early centuries. For this serves to keep the paradigm alive as an example and stimulus for the rest of the community. Understandably, this sort of thing will not be without its problems and difficulties, but what is at stake is too important for the experiment to be ruled out. If no communities, or only very few, celebrate the Easter vigil as is laid down in its complete form one can only fear that it will soon end up as a fine reform that never left the drawing-board.

In any case, however, the decisive role, as I said, must be played by the ministry of the word. If the Easter liturgy is the Church's great introduction to the mysteries, the celebrant, be he bishop or priest, must himself be the instructor! Incredible are the fruits, in the people who are present, of a homily well done, which brings the Word of God and the mystery celebrated close to the listeners' experience. This is the big chance for the renewed, post-conciliar liturgy. The reflections which I have unfolded to this point will, I hope, serve in their poor way also to this end: to make future priests fall in love with the marvelous task of being "stewards of the mysteries of God" (1 Cor 4:1), by turning their interest in theological study in this direction. In the gospel, Jesus speaks of "the faithful and prudent servant whom the master has put in charge of his household to distribute their food at the proper time" and says of him: "Blessed is that servant!" (cf. Matt 24:45f.).

NOTES

1. St. Ambrose, *De mysteriis* 1:1 (CSEL 73, p. 89).
2. St. Augustine, *Epistola* 55.11.21 (CSEL 34, p. 192).
3. St. Cyril of Jerusalem, *Catechesis mystagogica* 1.1 (PG 33, 1066).
4. St. Ambrose, *De sacramentis* 1.2f (CSEL 73, p. 15f.).
5. *Pesachim* 10.5.
6. Philo, *De congressu eruditionis gratia* 106.
7. *Commentarium in Iohannis Evangelium* 10.110 (GCS 4, p. 189).
8. Cf. Origen, *In Numeros homilia* 23.6 (GCS 7, p. 218).
9. Asterius Sophista, *Homily on Psalm 5,* 6.4 (*Asterii Sophistae quae supersunt,* Oslo 1956, p. 77).
10. *Exsultet* 4.
11. Cf. H. de Lubac, *Exegese medievale: Les quatre sens de l'Ecriture,* Paris 1959, 1/1, p. 305–27.
12. Melito of Sardis, *On Pascha* 6–7 (SCh 123, p. 62).
13. Cf. ibid., 36–37.
14. See "Notes on the correct way to present the Jews and Judaism in preaching and catechesis in the Roman Catholic Church," issued by the Secretariat for Promoting Christian Unity, May 1985.
15. *Exsultet* 5.

16. St. Augustine, *Sermo* 216.5 (PL 38, 1079).
17. Cf. St. Anselm, *Cur Deus homo?* 2.18, 20; St. Thomas Aquinas, *Summa theologiae* 3.46.1 ad 3.
18. *Exsultet* 3.
19. J.-B. Bossuet, *Oeuvres complètes* Paris 1836, 4, p. 365.
20. *Exsultet* 5.
21. *Ancient paschal homily* 17 (SCh 27, p. 145).
22. Philo, *De specialibus legibus* 2.151.
23. *Targum on Exodus* 12:42.
24. St. Cyril of Jerusalem, *Catechesis* 14.10 (PG 33, 836).
25. *Paschal homily* 27 (SCh 48, p. 135).
26. Cf. ibid., 28.
27. *Exsultet* 1.
28. Ibid., 5.
29. Ibid.
30. St. Ambrose, *In Psalmos* 39.20 (CSEL 64, p. 225).
31. St. Ambrose, *De Iacob,* 1.6.21 (CSEL 32, 2, p. 18).
32. Cf. St. Augustine, *Enchiridion* 11 (PL 40, 236).
33. Dame Julian of Norwich, *Revelations,* chapter 27.
34. St. Gregory of Nyssa, *Oratio catechetica* 32 (PG 45, 80).
35. Melito of Sardis, *On Pascha* 66 (SCh 123, p. 96).
36. *Ancient paschal homily* 62 (SCh 27, p. 189).
37. *Easter Stichira.*
38. St. Gregory Nazianzen, *Oratio* 45.30 (PG 36, 664).

Chapter Six

"Purify Yourselves from the Old Yeast"

The Paschal Mystery in Life (1)

I said in the previous pages that Christ's Passover is prolonged in the Church, taking place on two different planes: liturgical-sacramental and personal or existential. Let us now talk about this second plane; at last, let us talk about the paschal mystery in life. The biblical text in which this more personal plane of the Passover is best set forth is 1 Corinthians 5:7: "Clear out the old yeast, so that you may become a fresh batch of dough, inasmuch as you are unleavened. For our paschal lamb, Christ, has been sacrificed." We have thus arrived at that famous "Passover of Human Nature" which, in the Bible from the earliest times accompanies the "Passover of God" and which the Fathers defined as a passing from vice to virtue, from sin to grace. The language used by the Apostle in the passage I have just quoted recalls a Jewish custom. The day before the Passover, Jewish women, in obedience to the ordinance in Exodus 12:15, would scour their entire house, scrutinizing every corner by candlelight, to seek and get rid of every tiniest scrap of leavened bread, so that the feast could then be celebrated with unleavened bread only. (Something of the like passed into Christian tradition too; so, in Christian households, especially in the countryside, it used to be the custom, at least until a few years ago, to have a grand spring-cleaning in which crockery or other household articles that were damaged or worn out were thrown away, so that everything would be whole and new for Easter.) Well, the Apostle draws his idea from the Jewish custom, in order to illustrate the moral implications of the Christian Passover; it is to be seen as symbolic. Believers themselves must scrutinize the inner house of the heart, so as to destroy everything pertaining to the old regime of sin and corruption and to be able to celebrate the feast "with the unleavened bread of sincerity and truth'' (1 Cor 5:8), that is to say, in purity and holiness, and with no longer any link with sin. There is, in a word, a spring-cleaning of heart and life for Easter, which all are invited to perform if they really wish to enter the light of Easter.

There is a very close nexus, a logical consequence, between Christ's sacrifice and the moral commitment of the Christian: because Christ has been sacrificed as our paschal lamb, we ought to purify ourselves. The great Easter text of Romans 6:1ff. insists on this connection: If Christ died for all, then by the same token, all have died (cf. also 2 Cor 5:14). That is to say: if Christ has died to sin, then all have properly speaking died to sin; if Christ has risen from the dead, then all of us ought to "walk in newness of life," as people who, in hope, have already risen again.

These passages resound to the great Pauline intuition that we are not saved *because* of our works but neither are we saved *without* our works. What actually saves us is Christ's Passover, that is to say, his sacrifice and resurrection; but Christ's Passover is not efficacious for us unless it becomes "our" Passover. Moral and ascetic commitment is not the *cause* of salvation; it does, however, have to be the *effect* of it. I do not purify myself from sin in order to be saved; but, I purify myself from sin because I have been saved, because Christ has been sacrificed for my sins! The contrary—that is, to go on living in my sins—is "absurd": that is, like claiming to be alive to grace and to sin, alive and dead, free and enslaved, at the same time (cf. Rom 6:2, 15ff.).

1. *"I shall remove the heart of stone from your bodies"*

If we look a little closer at the two paschal passages just mentioned (1 Cor 5:7 and Rom 6:1f.), we shall find two key words in them with which the Apostle sums up all the moral consequences that flow from Christ's Passover: *purification* and *newness*. *"Purify yourselves* from the old yeast, so as to be a *new* dough.'' The former is placed more directly in relationship with Christ's death, the latter with Christ's resurrection. Christ has been sacrificed: purify yourselves! Christ has risen from the dead: walk in newness of life! These two ideas are not separate or juxtaposed but intimately connected. The first leads to the second, since no newness of life is possible without purification from sin. Let us therefore start by reflecting on this first aspect of our Passover: purification from sin.

This, I believe, is the Passover the Lord Jesus forcefully and brokenheartedly urges us to effect: to leave sin behind and purify ourselves from the old yeast, the yeast of the old Adam. All of us without exception must effect this "passing," since all of us are, to greater or lesser degree, involved in this sad reality: "If we say we are without sin, we deceive ourselves, and the truth is not in us. If we acknowledge our sins, he is faithful and just and will forgive our sins and cleanse us from all wrong-doing" (1 John 1:8-9).

But what sin are we talking about? What is the "sin" that we have to "acknowledge"? Certainly, first of all it means the actual sins we commit every day, for "we all fall short in many respects," St. James reminds us (Jas 3:2). But if we stop here, we shall only be touching the consequences and staying very much on the surface. St. John the Evangelist more often speaks of sin in the singular than in the plural: "the sin of the world," "if we say we are without sin. . . ." St. Paul draws a clear distinction between sin as a state of sinfulness ("sin that dwells in me," Rom 7:17) and the sins that are its external manifestations, much as the fiery heart of a volcano is distinct from the eruptions which every so often it causes on the outside. He says, "Sin must not reign over your mortal bodies, so that you obey their desires. And do not present the parts of your bodies to sin as weapons for wickedness" (Rom 6:12-13). This sin in the singular the Apostle represents as a "king" hidden in the recesses of his palace, who rules by means of his emissaries (the desires) and his instruments (our limbs).

So it is not enough to attack the various sins we commit day by day. This would be like putting the axe to the branches rather than to the root and would achieve virtually nothing. Those of us who might be content to do this and, each time we examine our conscience, patiently pass our sins in review so as to confess them in the sacrament of reconciliation without ever going any deeper, would be like that inept farmer who, instead of digging up the couch grass, comes along from time to time and picks off the flower spikes.

As regards sin, therefore, there is a more radical operation to be performed; only they who perform this operation truly make their Passover, and the operation consists in "making a clean break with sin" (cf. 1 Pet 4:1), by destroying the very body of sin (cf. Rom 6:6).

Let me explain what I mean by an example, or rather tell you about a small experience of my own. I was alone, reciting the psalm that says: "LORD, you have probed me and you know me . . . you understand my thoughts from afar . . . with all my ways you are familiar" (Ps 139:1f.). Suddenly I seemed to be seeing myself from God's point of view, as if I were scrutinizing myself through his eyes. In my mind there formed the very clear image of a stalagmite, one of those columns that form in the depths of certain caves owing to drops of calcareous water falling from the roof. At the same time I had the explanation of this unusual image. My actual sins over the years have fallen on to the floor of my heart like so many drops of calcareous water. Each of them has deposited a little calcareous material, that is to say, something opaque, hard, and resistant to God, adding to what was already there. Most of this fell away from time to time, thanks to confessions, Eucharists, prayer. But on each occasion, something remained "unmelted," and this was because repentance and contrition were never total, never absolute. And so my stalagmite grew like a "column of infamy" inside me; it became like a large stone, weighing me down and obstructing me in my spiritual activities, as though I were, spiritually speaking, in a plaster cast.

This is, exactly, that "body of sin" of which St. Paul speaks, that "old yeast" which, if not gotten rid of, will inject an element of corruption into our every action and obstruct the way to holiness. What is to be done about it? We cannot remove the stalagmite by our own will alone, since it is actually in our will! It is our old "me"; it is our self-regard; it is literally our "stony heart" (Ezek 11:19). The only thing left for us to do is pray. To beg the Lamb of God who takes away the sins of the world to take ours away too. We have seen what pain Jesus underwent for us to become children of God, and what our wrongdoings have done to Jesus in return. Happy are we if the Holy Spirit inspires our hearts with desire for a new, different, and stronger contrition than heretofore: a desire to dissolve our sins once and for all in tears, if we have never done that. Those of us who have not as yet experienced the savor of these tears, such as the saints have shed, should allow ourselves no peace until we have obtained this from the Holy Spirit (for it is indeed a gift of the Holy Spirit). "No one can enter the kingdom of God," Jesus said to Nicodemus, "without being born of water and Spirit" (Jn 3:5). Once we have been through the waters of baptism, there are no other waters than the waters of contrition by which we may be reborn. From tears like these, really new human beings emerge like newborn children (cf. 1 Pet 2:2), ready to serve God in a new way, since free henceforth from the shackles of sin. This is not supererogatory; this is obligatory. "Unless you turn and become like children," these children born of repentance and contrition, "you will not enter the kingdom of heaven"(Matt 18:3).

When the Lord inspires us with an ardent desire for total purification from sin, the entire Bible immediately takes on new meaning for us, since it was written in great part for this purpose: to help us become aware of our sinfulness and seek to be free of it. We pray with the Bible. The psalms teach us to pray to be purified from sin:

> Cleanse me of sin with hyssop, that I may be purified;
> wash me and I shall be whiter than snow. . . .
> A clean heart create for me, O God. . . .
> My sacrifice, O God, is a contrite spirit (Ps 51:9, 12, 19).

The prophets teach us to hope for this: "I will sprinkle clean water upon you to cleanse you . . . I will give you a new heart and place a new spirit within you, taking from your bodies your stony hearts and giving you natural hearts" (Ezek 36:25-26). And, at last, Jesus Christ offers it to us as an accomplished fact, as the fruit of his sacrifice: "Christ loved the Church and handed himself over for her to sanctify her, cleansing her by the bath of water with the word so that he might present to himself the Church in splendor, without spot or wrinkle or any such thing, that she might be holy and without blemish" (Eph 5:25-27).

What Jesus has done for the Church as a whole, he has also done for every individual; what he desires of the Church as a whole—that she be holy and without blemish—he also desires of those individuals consecrated to him, of priests, to whom he once said: "Purify yourselves, you who carry the vessels of the LORD" (Isa 52:11). (Always this word "purify yourselves," "be purified"!) For the Thursday following Ash Wednesday, the divine office bids us listen to these words of St. Leo the Great:

> Now, as we come closer to the season which is specially marked
> by the mysteries of our redemption, the days leading up to the

festival of Easter, the need for our religious preparation is ever more insistently proclaimed. The special feature of Easter is that it is the occasion when the whole Church rejoices over the forgiveness of sin. This forgiveness takes place, not only in the case of those who are freshly reborn through baptism, but also in the case of us others who for some time have been counted among God's adopted children. Certainly it is true that the water of rebirth initially brings about our new life of grace, but for all of us it is still necessary to struggle every day against the rust of our earthly nature. Whatever steps forward we make, there is not one of us who is not always bound to do better. All of us must strive hard, and so on Easter Day no one should still be bound by the vices of his former nature."[1]

2. *Purification and renewal*

The word of God entrusts us therefore with an urgent appeal intended for all the Church's children; you must repent of your sins and free yourselves from sin. Christians no longer recognize their real enemy, the boss who keeps them enslaved, but this is because it is a gilded slavery. Many people who talk about sin have an utterly inadequate idea of what it is, having ended up basically identifying it with the position adopted by their own political or ideological opponents: sin is "right-wing"; sin is "left-wing." But equally true of the kingdom of sin is what Jesus said of the kingdom of God: When they tell you, sin is here, or sin is there, do not believe them: for sin is inside *you*" (cf. Luke 17:21).

As regards sin, many Christians, distracted by the mass media and the spirit of the age, have fallen into a kind of narcosis. They no longer notice it. They joke with the word *sin* as though it were the most harmless thing in the world, living with it fearlessly year after year. In fact, they no longer know what sin is. An inquiry into what our people think about sin would, I think, produce the most disconcerting results.

If we wish to carry the conciliar renewal of Church structures and guiding principles into the daily lives of believers, so as to renew them in holiness (which I believe to be the wish of all in the Church), we must "cry out full-throated and unsparingly," yes, today, "to tell the people their sins" (Isa 58:1f.), and first of all the sin of having forgotten God, or of having relegated him to last place in their own preoccupations. We must somehow manage to make them grasp the truth which is constantly being hammered home in the Bible, that *sin is death*. We too, like the prophets of Israel, must say: "Cast away from you all the crimes you have committed and make for yourselves a new heart and a new spirit. Why should you die, O house of Israel?" (Ezek 18:31); "where would you yet be struck, you that rebel again and again" (Isa 1:5).

When God speaks to us of repentance and purification from our sins, he does so because he wants us to be happy, not unhappy; he wants life, not death. So, it is a gift he makes to us, not a burden he imposes. An authentically Christian and evangelical penitential movement ought always to bear this positive imprint of love of life, of joy, of dash, as did the penitential movement started by St. Francis and his companions, who originally called themselves just "the penitents of Assisi." Sincere contrition is the safest route to "perfect joy." Sin is mainly responsible for the great unhappiness holding sway on earth.

Even so, the word which calls the world to repentance is an austere one. In order to be heard, those who proclaim it must proclaim it "in Spirit and in power," as the Apostle Peter did in his sermon on the day of Pentecost. Hearing him speak in this way, the Acts relate, those present felt "cut to the heart," and said, "What are we to do, my brothers?" Peter said, "Repent . . . and you will receive the gift of the Holy Spirit" (Acts 2:37-38).

Who will have the courage needed for directing this call to conversion to our brothers today? The word of God suggests an instrument which is indispensable for this task: a renewed priesthood which has itself "made a clean break" with sin. There is a page in the prophet Zechariah which has much impressed me, seeming as it does to have been written precisely for our present situation. The moment is shortly after the chosen people's return from the Exile; the rebuilding of the Temple in Jerusalem has just begun; everyone seems happy with the way things are going. But lo, God intervenes anew to point the way to another, more interior, more universal rebuilding, which has as its objective the holiness and integrity of the whole nation's religious life. In a word, here too attention shifts from the renewal of the structures and, as it were, the external framework of religion, to the renewal of spirit and heart. To achieve this purpose, the Lord intends first to renew the priesthood. The scene is a dramatic one. The high priest Joshua, representing the whole priesthood of Israel, stands before the Lord in the mourning garments of the Exile, signifying the general state of guilt and disobedience to God. Satan stands on his right to accuse him. But God pronounces this word over him: " 'Take off his filthy garments and clothe him in festal garments.' He also said, 'Put a clean miter on his head.' And they put a clean miter on his head and clothed him with the garments. Then the angel of the LORD said, 'See, I have taken away your guilt' " (Zech 3:4-5). Jesus took some of the imagery from this passage for his parable of the prodigal son.

May the Lord let us too soon hear that consoling word: "See, I have taken away your guilt!" Then it will truly be Easter for us, we shall have completed the "holy passage" and shall be able to claim for ourselves the words of the Jewish and Christian paschal liturgy:

> He has made us pass:
> from slavery to freedom,
> from sadness to joy,
> from mourning to the feast,
> from darkness to the light,
> from slavery to redemption.
> Therefore we say before him: Alleluia![2]

NOTES

1. Leo the Great, *Sermon 44 on Lent* 1 (CCL 138A, p. 258).
2. *Pesachim* 10.5; and Melito of Sardis, *On Pascha* 68 (SCh 123, p. 96).

Chapter Seven

"Return into Yourself"

The Paschal Mystery in Life (2)

Let us set out again from that passage in St. Paul, where the Christian Passover is mentioned for the first time. Though brief, it says much. "Clear out the old yeast, so that you may become a fresh batch of dough, inasmuch as you are unleavened. For our paschal lamb, Christ, has been sacrificed! Therefore, let us celebrate the feast, not with the old yeast, the yeast of malice and wickedness, but with the unleavened bread of sincerity and truth" (1 Cor 5:7-8).

In point of fact, this passage speaks of two different Passovers: Christ's Passover which consists in his sacrifice, and the individual Christian's Passover which consists in passing from the old to the new, from the corruption of sin to purity of life. Christ's Passover is already "done"; the verb in this case is in the past tense: "has been sacrificed." As far as we are concerned, we only have to believe it and to celebrate it. The individual Christian's Passover, on the other hand, is all "to be done"; the verbs in this case are in the imperative: "purify yourselves, let us celebrate."

In the Christian environment we find again the characteristic dialectic between God's Passover and human Passover. And this distinction in turn reflects other distinctions better known and general: those between *kerygma* and *paraenesis*; between faith and works, between grace and freedom, between Christ-the-gift and Christ-the-exemplar. God's Passover, now achieved in the person of Christ, is the object of the *kerygma*; it is a gift of grace, received by faith and always efficacious in itself. The human Passover is the object of the *paraenesis;* it is effected by works and imitation, it postulates freewill, it depends on the dispositions of the individual concerned. The Passover thus appears as the concentrate of all salvation history: in it are reflected all the

92

lines and structures relevant to the entire biblical revelation and to all Christian existence.

The tradition of the Church has comprehended and developed this tension between the two dimensions of revelation by distinguishing two components or fundamental senses within the overall spiritual sense of the Bible: the typological sense and the tropological sense. *Typology* (which St. Paul in Galatians 4:24 calls *allegory*) is when a fact in the Old Testament—a word or action as it may be—is explained as referring to another fact in the New Testament concerning Christ or the Church. The *tropological* or moral sense is when a fact, be it in the Old or the New Testament, is explained in terms of "what has to be done." In a later period, when theology began to be differentiated into independent treatises, the typological or allegorical sense became the province of dogmatic theology, while the moral sense became that of moral and spiritual theology.

This patristic and medieval doctrine of the three, or four, different levels and senses of Scripture has often been regarded with suspicion and pushed aside in recent times, but it is founded, as few other theories are, in the New Testament itself. To reject it *en bloc*, or to deny its very legitimacy, means discrediting *en bloc* and defining as "childish" the way in which the apostles interpreted the Scriptures and, more significantly still, how Jesus Christ himself did. Let us take a single example which shows how these three senses of Scripture are clearly present when St. Paul explains the events of the Passover in 1 Corinthians 10:1f.

(a) *The historical or literal sense*: "Our ancestors were all under the cloud and all passed through the sea" (10:1);

(b) *The typological or allegorical sense*: That rock was Christ; "all were baptized into Moses in the cloud and in the sea, all ate the same spiritual food and all drank the same spiritual drink" (10:2-4). The events of the Exodus are seen as figures (*typoi*) of Christ and of the sacraments of the Church, baptism and Eucharist (cf. 1 Cor 12:13);

(c) *The moral sense:* "These things happened as examples for us, so that we might not desire evil things . . . and not become idolaters . . . not indulge in immorality . . . not grumble" (10:6f.).

We shall also find this method of interpretation being applied in the New Testament to concrete realities and institutions, for instance, to the Temple. In the historical sense, the Temple means Solomon's Temple; in the typological or allegorical sense it is Jesus

Christ, the new temple (cf. John 2:19); in the moral and personal sense it is every believing soul (cf. 1 Cor 3:16). So one cannot *en bloc*, either in principle or in concrete application, reject this method of interpretation used by the Fathers, without, in so doing, discrediting the method of interpreting the Bible which is used throughout the New Testament.

1. *"Return to the heart"*

Two characteristics, or rules, govern the moral interpretation of the Old Testament and of all Scripture: first, that which has happened once (*semel*) must be repeated every day (*quotidie*); second, what has happened for all in a visible and material manner must happen in each in an interior and personal manner. These two rules can be summed up in two words: *actualization* and *interiorization*. In my view, that kind of modern exegesis known as kerygmatic or existential has reached the same conclusion by another route, in its insistence on the "for me" and on the "here and now" (*hic et nunc*) of the word of God.

Let us now apply all this to the Passover. How can we conceive of this daily, personal, interior Passover? In the previous chapter, I already illustrated one aspect of this moral or human Passover, the one consisting in purification from the old yeast of sin. Now I should like to take a step forward and show how Passover spirituality is not confined to the first, negative content, being the flight from sin, but also throws its light on what comes after, that is, the road to holiness.

Biblical and patristic tradition has interpreted the paschal idea of "passing" in various ways: as "passing over" (*hyperbasis*), as "passing across" (*diabasis*), as "passing upward" (*anabasis*), as "passing out" (*exodus*), as "passing forward" (*progressio*) and in certain cases as "passing back" (*reditus*). The Passover is a passing "over" when it means God's passing, sparing and protecting; it is a passing "across" when it refers to the Israelites' passing from Egypt to the Promised Land, from slavery to freedom; it is a passing "upward" when a human being passes from the things of here below to those above; it is a passing "out" when the individual emerges from sin or quits slavery; it is a passing "forward" when we make progress in holiness and goodness; lastly, it is a passing "back" when we pass from the old Adam to spiritual youth, when we "return" to our origins and re-enter our lost paradise.

These were all modulations of the notion of Passover corresponding to the thought patterns and needs of their own day. Today I think we ought to take a new nuance of this paschal dynamism on board, a new notion of "passing": "passing inwards," introversion or interiorization. The passing from the outward to the inward, from the outside to the inside of ourselves. From the Egypt of dispersion and dissipation to the Promised Land of the heart. There exists an "esoteric" Passover in the most positive sense of the word, that is to say, a Passover that goes on within, in secret or tending to the inward. A Passover, in a word, which is centripetal and not centrifugal. And this is the Passover I want to deal with in this chapter.

Special Passovers are celebrated in the Church from time to time: the Passover of the workers, of the sick, of the students . . . To these I should like to add the Passover of the inner self, "of the hidden character of the heart," as Scripture calls it (cf. 1 Pet 3:4). In Deuteronomy we find the following regulation concerning Passover: "You may not celebrate the Passover wherever you please, but will sacrifice the Passover only where the Lord chooses to be the dwelling place of his name" (cf. Deut 16:5-6). What is this place the Lord chooses? Long ago it was Solomon's Temple, the historic Temple; now, as we have seen, it is the spiritual or personal temple, the believer's heart. "For we are the temple of the living God" (2 Cor 6:16). This is really where the true Passover is celebrated, without which all the others remain incomplete and ineffective.

Our present-day culture no longer reasons so much in terms of here below, on high; down here, up there; on earth, in heaven, as rather with the modern thought pattern of object, subject; nature, spirit. And this is very much like talking of what is outside us and what, by contrast, is in us. In this sense, interiorizing the Passover also means actualizing it, making it meaningful for our own day and contemporaries. So the Passover, like all the great realities in the Bible, is an "open structure," capable of acquiring new content and meeting new challenges. As Scripture "grows with the growth of those who read it,"[1] so the Passover grows with the growth of those who celebrate it.

What this "passing inwards" involves we shall get St. Augustine to explain, who in this case as in many another seems to be the first of the moderns. In an address to his people, he comments on a verse in the prophet Isaiah which, in the version he was using said: "Return, you transgressors, to the heart (*redite, praevaricatores, ad cor*)" (Isa 46:8). At a certain point he launches this passionate appeal:

> Return to the heart! Why do you go away from yourselves, and perish from yourselves? Why do you go the ways of solitude? Your wanderings have led you astray. Return! Where? To the Lord. It is quickly done! First, return to your heart. You are wandering outside, an exile from yourself; you do not know yourself and you ask who made you! Return, return to the heart; detach yourself from the body. . . . Return to your heart! There examine what perhaps you perceive about God, for God's image is there. Christ dwells in the inner self; in the inner self you will be renewed in the image of God.[2]

If we want a concrete image or a symbol to help us achieve this conversion to the inward, the gospel offers us one with the episode of Zacchaeus. Zacchaeus is the man who wants to know what Jesus is like and, to do this, comes out of his house, worms his way through the crowd and climbs up into a tree. He seeks him outside. But Jesus going by sees him and says to him: "Zacchaeus, come down quickly, for today I must stay at your house" (Luke 19:5). Jesus goes home with Zacchaeus and there, in private, without witnesses, the miracle occurs: Zacchaeus realizes exactly who Jesus is and finds salvation. We are often like Zacchaeus. We go in search of Jesus, we go looking for him outside, through the streets, among the crowds. And Jesus himself invites us to go home, into our own heart, where he wants to meet us.

2. *The interior life: a value under threat*

There is a reason for this insistence on the Passover of the inner self: the inner life is under threat. The phrase "interior life" which used to be used more or less synonymously with "spiritual life," now tends to be regarded with suspicion. There are dictionaries of spirituality now which omit the lemmata "interior life" and "recollection" altogether, while those that do give express reservations about them. For instance, the point is made that, all said and done, there is no biblical term corresponding exactly to these words; that, on this matter, the determining influence of Platonic philosophy could have been at work; that it could encourage subjectivism. . . . A telling symptom of this decline in taste and esteem for the inner life is the fate that has overtaken *The Imitation of Christ*, which is a kind of introductory handbook to it. From being the book best loved by Christians after the Bible, it has become, in thirty years or so, one of the books least loved and least read.

Some of the reasons for this crisis are ancient ones, inherent in our own nature. Our makeup, or nature, consisting of body and spirit, makes us like an inclined plane, tilting outwards towards the visible and the multiplex. Like the universe, after the initial explosion (the famous Big Bang), we too are in a process of expansion and of retreating further and further from the center. "The eye is not satisfied with seeing, / nor is the ear filled with hearing," says Scripture (Eccl 1:8). We are perennially going out through the five doors or windows of our senses.

Other reasons, however, are more specific and contemporary. One is the emergence of the social, which is certainly a positive value of our times but which, if not brought back into equilibrium, can accentuate projection towards the external and depersonalization of the individual. In the secularized and lay culture of our day, the role the Christian interior life used to discharge has been assumed by psychology and psychoanalysis; these, however, go no further than the unconscious mind and subjective states, leaving the intimate link between human personality and God out of consideration.

In the ecclesiastical field, the affirmation under council auspices of the notion of a "Church for the world" has resulted in the old ideal of flight *from* the world being replaced by the ideal of flight *to* the world. This forsaking of the interior life and projection towards the external is an aspect—and one of the most dangerous—of the phenomenon of secularism. There has even been an attempt theologically to justify this new orientation, which goes by the name of theology of the death of God, or of the secular city. God, it is said, has himself set us the example. By becoming incarnate, he has emptied himself, come out of himself, out of trinitarian interiority, and become merged in the world; he has melted into the profane, has become a God dispossessed of self.

As always, when a traditional value goes into crisis, Christianity's response has to be to recapitulate, that is to say to take things back to their beginning, in order to carry them forward to function anew. In other words, we must set out again from the word of God and, by its light, rediscover within the same tradition that vital and perennial element, while freeing ourselves of those fallen elements in which it has been presented over the centuries. This was the method the Second Vatican Council adopted in all its labors. As in nature, in springtime, the tree is pruned of the previous season's branches to make it possible for the trunk to flower anew, so too we have to act in the life of the Church.

3. *Interior life in the Bible*

What do we find about the interior life in the Bible? Let us run over a few of the more significant facts.

Long ago, the prophets of Israel strove to displace the nation's interest from external and ritual religious practices to the inner life of a living relationship with God. "This people," we read in Isaiah, "draws near with words only and honors me with their lips alone, though their hearts are far from me and their reverence for me has become a routine observance of human precepts" (Isa 29:13). And this is why: "Man sees the appearance but the LORD looks into the heart" (1 Sam 16:7). "Rend your hearts, not your garments," we read in another of the prophets (Joel 2:13).

This is the type of religious reform that Jesus also preached and effected. Dogmatic preoccupations aside, anyone who examines Jesus' actions and words from the standpoint of the history of religions observes one thing above all: that he was trying to renew the Jewish religious spirit, which had largely dried up in ritualism and legalism, by replacing an intimate and loving relationship with God at the center of it. He never tires of recalling his countrymen to that secret place, the heart, where true contact with God and with his living will takes place and on which the value of every action depends (cf. Matt 15:10f.).

The profound reasons that Jesus gives for this are that "God is Spirit and those who worship him must worship in Spirit and Truth" (John 4:24). This sentence has different levels of meaning, down to the deepest of all, in which "Spirit and Truth" mean the Holy Spirit and the Word, God himself and his living reality. But certainly among the various levels there is one where "spirit and truth" mean the inner self, spiritual awareness, the spiritual temple as opposed to external places, such as in Jesus' time were the Temple in Jerusalem and the one on Mount Gerizim. Just as, in order to make contact with the world, which is material, we need to pass by way of our body, so to make contact with God, who is Spirit, we need to pass by way of our heart and our soul, which is spirit.

Jesus often mentions another reason. What is done outwardly is exposed to the almost inevitable risk of hypocrisy. Other people's attention has the power to deflect our intention, just as certain magnetic fields can deflect rays. Our activity loses its genuineness and its reward. Appearing takes the upper hand over being. This being so, Jesus invites us to give alms in private, to pray to the Father "in secret" (cf. Matt 6:1-4). True, we are not yet at the modern idea of the secret inner life or of selfconsciousness, but we are certainly going in that direction. St. Ambrose is therefore far from wrong when, explaining the passage where Jesus invites us to retire into our own room and close the door in order to pray to the Father, he comments: "Do not suppose that this room is only the room enclosed by walls; it is also the room which is within yourself, in which your thoughts are contained and where all your affections dwell."[3]

Lastly, the call to the interior life finds its deepest and most objective biblical motivation in the doctrine of the indwelling of God, Father, Son, and Holy Spirit, in the soul: a doctrine developed alike by St. Paul and St. John (John 14:17, 23; Rom 5:5; Gal 4:6).

Imposed on this gospel background, we find the notion of the "inner self" or of the "hidden character of the heart," about which we so often read in the New Testament (cf. Rom 7:22; 2 Cor 4:16; 1 Pet 3:4).

What has Greek philosophy and particularly Platonism added to all this? Plato too had launched the program of an interior life, inviting us to practice recollection, to concentrate our minds, to withdraw from the dispersion of the world and our own bodies.[4] His disciple Plotinus took up and developed the program. In the treatise *On the Good or the One*, he speaks of a "silent entering into isolation, in a state that is immune to shocks," of a "going inwards, of penetrating the inner sanctum of oneself."[5]

But does all this add anything new to the gospel message? No, nothing except a useful means of expression for bringing the biblical message closer to the Hellenistic culture of the day, which was characterized by a much sharper distinction between soul and body than is to be found in the Bible. It also brought an enrichment and a precise definition at the level of expression and symbols. The Fathers continued along the same line as St. Paul's address in Athens: "What you have glimpsed and have blindly groped for, we proclaim to you as something that has already come to pass" (cf. Acts 17:23). But they brought much more that was new to the Platonic doctrine of the inner life than they ever acquired from it. The greatest novelty was this: turning back into the self, human beings find God; not some generalized, impersonal God but the God revealed in Christ. They find not only their own spirit but the Holy Spirit. "Do not come out, return into yourself," St. Augustine exhorts us. "Truth dwells in the inner self."[6] But we have already heard who this truth is for him, in that passage already quoted where he said: "Christ dwells in the inner self."[7] This does not come from Plotinus but from St. Paul, who had spoken about Christ's dwelling in our hearts through faith (cf. Eph 3:17).

For Plotinus, the withdrawal into the self is a process of ascent to unity. It resembles the movement of the radii which, proceeding from the circumference to the center, gradually get closer and closer to one another until they converge. But following this way, what do we find at the center? Just a point, homogeneous with everything else, therefore the One. What, however, is found when, following St. Augustine, we arrive at the center, at the heart? Not a point or an impersonal unity, but a person, a "you": Jesus Christ! Between the pagan and the Christian inner life the gap is infinite. The latter has been rightly defined as an "objective inner life." When we withdraw into ourselves, we find not only ourselves, our true "we," but we also find the Other *par excellence*, who is God. The Christian interior life is not a form of subjectivism, but the cure for it.

I said the Passover is the passing from outside oneself to inside oneself. Certainly the true and final Passover does not consist in withdrawing into oneself but in coming out of oneself; not in finding oneself, but in losing oneself, in denying oneself. Having reached the end of his book *The Soul's Journey into God*, St. Bonaventure writes: "It now remains for our mind, by contemplating these things, to transcend and pass over not only this sense-world but even itself. In this passing over, Christ is the way and the door, Christ is the ladder and the vehicle."[8] Yet we have to retire into ourselves in order to transcend ourselves. St. Bonaventure illustrates this, taking Solomon's Temple as his example. To enter the holy of holies, one had first to cross the external threshold of the Temple and enter the holy place. For only from here, from inside, could one reach the holy of holies and the face of God.[9] Only at the end of this road can the true moral or mystical Passover be celebrated. This takes place, St. Bonaventure says, when "turning in faith, hope and love, devotion, admiration, exultation, appreciation, praise, and joy, to Christ hanging on the cross, we make the Pasch, that is, the Passover with Christ. By the staff of the cross, we pass over the Red Sea, going from Egypt into the desert, where we shall taste the hidden manna and rest in the tomb with Christ, being dead to the outer world."[10]

This was already implicit in St. Augustine's cry: "Return into yourself!" which continued: "If you return into yourself, you will discover that you too are mutable; you will transcend yourself too. But remember, in transcending yourself, you will be transcending your own faculty of thought. Aim, therefore, at that point where the very light of reason is kindled."[11] On the same plane as the aim of discovering God, St. Augustine put the two movements which consist "either in ascending from the baser to the higher, or in withdrawing from outward things to those within."[12]

It must be admitted that, with the passing of time, aspects of this classic vision of Christian inwardness became dimmed, contributing to the crisis of which I have already spoken.[13] In certain currents of spirituality, as, for instance, in some of the Rhineland mystics, the objective character of this inner life became obscured. They insisted on return to the "depths of the soul" by means of what they called "introversion." But it does not always seem clear whether the depths of the soul pertain to the reality of God or to that of the I, or even worse, to both pantheistically fused together. The objective inner life becomes either entirely objective, when God replaces the I (pantheism), or entirely subjective, when the I replaces God (atheism).

In recent centuries the aspect of *method* has come to prevail over the *content* of Christian interior life, sometimes reducing it to a kind of technique of concentration and meditation, instead of being the encounter with the living Christ in one's heart; even though no period has been without its own magnificent achievements in Christian interior life. Blessed Elizabeth of the Trinity belongs to the category of purest objective inwardness, where she writes: "I have found paradise on earth, since paradise is God and God is in my heart."[14]

4. *Return to the interior life*

Let us linger no longer over the past but turn our attention to the present. Why is it so urgent to start talking about interior life again and rediscovering the taste for it? We live in a civilization entirely projected towards the external, outwards. We send our space probes to the edge of the solar system but for the most part do not know what there is in our own heart. Escaping, that is to say getting out, is a kind of watchword. We have escapist literature, escapist shows. Escapism has, one might say, become institutionalized. In contrast to this, words indicating a conversion to the inner life, such as introversion, have acquired a potentially negative meaning. The introvert is regarded as someone who has retreated into himself or herself. Silence strikes terror. People cannot live, work, study without talk or music as a background. There is a kind of *horror vacui,* fear of the void, prompting people to befuddle their senses. Never be on your own: that is the important thing.

I once had occasion to set foot in a discotheque, having been invited to talk to the young people attending it. That once was more than sufficient to make me aware of what goes on in such places: the orgy of noise, the deafening racket like a drug. I asked some of the young people as they came out of the disco, "Why do you all come here?" To this some replied, "So as not to have to think!" But to what manipulation are not such young people exposed, once they have given up thinking? "Weigh the work out to these people and keep them busy, so that they will not realize what Moses says is true" was the Egyptian Pharaoh's order (cf. Exod 5:9). The tacit though no less peremptory order of the modern pharaohs is: "Weigh out the noise to these young people, befuddle them with it, so that they will not think, will not make free choices, but follow the fashion that suits us, buy what we sell, think what we wish!" For a very influential sector of our society, that of show business and advertising, individuals count merely insofar as they are spectators, numbers to bump up program ratings.

We must oppose this progressive deprivation with a resolute No! The young are also very noble-hearted and ready to rebel against enslavement, and indeed there are hosts of young people who react against this assault and, as well as fleeing from it, seek out places and times for silence and contemplation every so often, so as to rediscover themselves and God within them. These are the young who have discovered the difference between being simply spectators and being contemplatives. In reverse, they have overcome the "sound barrier," this terrible barrier between the self and God.

Inner life is the way to a genuine life. People talk a lot today about genuineness, making it the criterion of success or failure in life. But where does this authenticity lie for the Christian? When is a young person truly himself or herself? Only when God is accepted as the measure. "A herdsman who (if this were possible) is a self only in the sight of cows is a very low self, and so also is a ruler who is a self in the sight of slaves—for in both cases the scale or measure is lacking. . . . But what an infinite accent falls upon the self by having God as a measure!"[15] "So much is said," writes the philosopher just quoted, "about wasted lives; but only that man's life is wasted who never . . . in the deepest sense received an impression of the fact that there is a God, and that he, he himself, his self, stands in this God's presence."[16] True it is that in solitude we are least alone!

In the light of these words I should like to say to many of the young: Young people, do not settle for just being "herdsmen"; aspire to becoming that wonderful thing: "a self standing in God's presence!"

The gospel tells us the story of a young "herdsman" who one day had the guts to make the break. He had run away from his father's house and wasted his possessions and his youth in riotous living. But one day "he came to himself." He reviewed his life, thought out what he would say and set off for home (cf. Luke 15:17). His conversion occurred at that moment, before setting out, while he was on his own in the middle of a herd of pigs. It occurred at the moment when, it is written, "he came to himself." Afterwards he simply carried out what he had decided. The outward conversion had been preceded by the inner one, which made it effective. What fruitfulness in that "coming to himself"!

I do not know if St. Augustine had those words of the gospel in mind when he uttered the invitation "Return to yourself!" but the prodigal son had certainly put that cry into practice before the saint built it into his teaching.

The young are not the only ones to be overwhelmed by the deluge of the external. It happens to the most committed and active members of the Church as well. Yes, members of religious orders too! Distraction is the name of the mortal illness likely to ensnare us all. We end up becoming like a garment turned inside-out, with our soul exposed to the four winds of heaven. In an address given to the superiors of a contemplative order, Paul VI said: "Today we live in a world seemingly in the grip of a fever which finds its way even into the sanctuary and into our solitude. Noise and uproar have invaded almost everything. People find it impossible now to practice recollection. Prey to a thousand distractions, they habitually waste their energies on the various forms assumed by modern culture. Newspapers, magazines, books invade the privacy of our homes and our hearts. It is harder than it used to be to find the opportunity for that recollectedness in which the soul manages to be fully engaged in God."

Nobody more than we needs to make the Passover of which we have just been speaking and which consists in conversion to the inner life. The absolute antithesis of this Passover is properly called distraction or escapism, or the turning back to the external. St. Teresa of Avila wrote a work, *The Interior Castle*, which is without a doubt one of the most mature fruits of Christian teaching about the inner life. But there also, alas, exists an "exterior castle" and today we realize it is possible to be shut up inside this castle too: shut out of our home, unable to get back into it; prisoners of the external world! This is how St. Augustine describes his own life before his conversion: "You were within me and I was outside, and there I sought for you and in my ugliness I plunged into the beauties that you have made. You were with me, and I was not with you. Those outer beauties kept me far from you, yet if they had not been in you, they would not have existed at all."[17] How many of us have to repeat that bitter confession: You were within me and I was outside!

Some people dream of solitude, but only dream about it. They love it, yet it remains a dream and is never translated into fact. In fact, they run away from it and are afraid of it. The vanishing of silence is a grave symptom. Those little cards which in every corridor of religious houses used to command in Latin, *Silentium!* have almost all been taken down. I believe that in many a religious environment, the dilemma looms: Silence or Death! Either an atmosphere and times for silence and the inner life are made available again, or progressive and complete spiritual destitution will follow. Jesus called hell the "outer darkness" (cf. Matt 8:12), and this description is highly significant.

We should not allow ourselves to be taken in by the usual objection: God is to be found outside, in our brothers and sisters, in the poor, in the struggle for justice; he is in the Eucharist, which is outside us, in the Word of God . . . All very true. But where do you truly encounter your brother, your sister, the poor, if not in your heart? If you only encounter them outside, you do not encounter individuals, persons, but things; you bump into them rather than meet them. Where do you encounter the Jesus of the Eucharist, if not in faith, that is to say, within yourself? A true encounter between persons can only occur between two awarenesses, two free wills, two inner lives.

The objection is also raised that, according to modern psychology, there are two categories of persons, two different human types: introverts and extroverts. The former find God within themselves; the latter, outside, in the cosmos or in other people. Of course, this distinction does exist and we are aware of it from daily experience. But this kind of difference cannot be applied so mechanically in the spiritual sphere. When God is concerned, a special consideration arises: God is Spirit! How, therefore, will you find him outside, in the cosmos, if not by retiring into yourself and opening the inner eye of faith? Also, in contemplating the cosmos and going towards other people, there must be—even if in differing measure and manner from one case to another—a habit of inwardness. If not, outside, in the cosmos and in beautiful creatures, we would no longer see God. We can throw ourselves on creatures and by them be carried far away from God, as St. Augustine has just reminded us. One may be an introverted type and find it hard to relate to other people and to approach one's neighbor, but one is not excused because of this from taking action, from discharging one's external duties. The same goes for the extrovert with regard to the claims of the inner life.

In any case, it would be a mistake to think that insistence on the inner life could harm our energetic commitment to the kingdom and to justice; to imagine, in other words, that to affirm the primacy of intention can be harmful to action. The inner life is not opposed to action but to a certain way of acting. Far from diminishing the importance of acting for God, interior life lays its foundations and keeps it going.

As frequently, when a spiritual or religious value goes into crisis, its *simulacrum*, which is the secular equivalent of that value, remains intact, so the secular or natural equivalent of the interior life is today called *introspection* in psychology and *concentration* in other spheres. Athletes and all those who are involved in undertakings requiring all their energies know how important concentration is. We all have a mental image of athletes completely self-absorbed, ready to dash forward to the winning post, as if they had to get in touch with a mysterious source of energy within them. The artist is the same; so is the conductor of an orchestra. Nothing is more harmful to an athlete or an artist than to have the mood of concentration broken, and it is precisely to this that subsequent failure is all too often ascribed. This is a pale reflection of what goes on in the spiritual field, of the importance of contemplation and recollection, from which action ought to spring.

If, therefore, we want to imitate what God has done, we must really imitate him all the way. True, he emptied himself, came out of himself, from the inner life of the Trinity, to come into the world. But we know how this came about. "That which he was, he remained; that which he was not, he assumed," runs an old maxim about the incarnation. Without leaving the Father's breast, the Word came among us. He was "all in himself and all in us."[18] So we too go towards the world but without ever at all coming out of ourselves. "The man of interior life," says *The Imitation of Christ*, "soon recollects himself because he never wholly pours himself forth on exterior things. Exterior labor is no prejudice to him, nor any employment necessary for the time; but as things happen, so he accommodates himself to them."[19]

5. *The hermit and his hermitage*

But let us also try to see what we should do, practically speaking, in order to recover and preserve the habit of interior life. Moses was a very active man. But we read that he had a portable tent made for himself and that at each stage of the Exodus he had the tent erected outside the encampment and regularly went into it to consult the Lord. There, "the LORD used to speak to Moses face to face, as one man speaks to another" (Exod 33:11).

But even this cannot always be done. He cannot always retire into a chapel or some lonely place in order to renew contact with God. For this reason St. Francis of Assisi suggests another device more within our reach. Sending his friars into the streets of the world, he said: We always have a hermitage with us wherever we go, and whenever we wish we can, like hermits, retire into this hermitage. "Brother Body is the hermitage and the soul is the hermit who lives inside, so as to pray to God and meditate."[20] Thus, in a form all his own, Francis resumes the ancient and traditional idea of the interior cell which we each carry with us, even when we go out and about, into which we may always retire with our thoughts, so as to re-establish a living contact with the Truth that dwells within us.

Mary is the human image of the Christian inner life. She who for nine months actually, physically carried the Word of God in her womb, "who conceived him in her heart before even in her body," is the very icon of the introverted soul, literally turned or drawn inwards. Of her it is said that she meditated on everything in her heart (cf. Luke 2:19). She interiorized it all, she lived it all within. How the Church needs to reflect this model! In this respect how seriously we should take the teaching of Vatican II, according to which Mary is the "type of the Church": what we observe in her, we should also be able to see in the Church.

To her we plead that we may make this new Passover which consists in passing from the outward to the inward, from noise to silence, from distraction to recollection, from dissipation of energy to unity, from the world to God.

NOTES

1. St. Gregory the Great, *Moralia* 20.1 (PL 76, 135).
2. St. Augustine, *In Iohannis Evangelium* 18.10 (CCL 36, p. 186).
3. St. Ambrose, *De Cain et Abel* 1.9 (CSEL 32, 1, p. 372).
4. Cf. Plato, *Phaedo* 67C; 83A.
5. Plotinus, *Enneads*, 6.9.
6. St. Augustine, *De vera religione* 39.72 (CCL 32, p. 234).
7. St. Augustine, *In Iohannis Evangelium* 18.10.

8. St. Bonaventure, *Itinerarium mentis in Deum* 7.1.
9. Ibid., 3.1; 5.1.
10. Ibid., 7.2.
11. St. Augustine, *De vera religione* 39.72.
12. St. Augustine, *De Trinitate* 14.3.5 (CCL 50A, 426).
13. Cf N. Nedoncelle, "Interiorité," in *Dictionnaire de Spiritualité* 7 (1970) coll. 1889–1903; cf. also M. Dupuy, "Introversion," coll. 1904–1918.
14. Bl. Elizabeth of the Trinity, *Letter* 107 to Mme De Sourdon (1902).
15. S. Kierkegaard, *The Sickness unto Death* 2.1.1.
16. Ibid.
17. St. Augustine, *Confessions* 10.27.
18. Cf. St. Leo the Great, *Epistola ad Flavianum* 3 (PL 54, 763).
19. *Imitation of Christ* 2.1.
20. *Legend of Perugia* 80 (*Writings,* cit. p. 1056).

Chapter Eight

"Go Forth from This World, O Christian Soul"

The Paschal Mystery in Death

"There is another figure in the Exodus from Egypt," writes Origen, "which is effected when the soul leaves the darkness of this world and the blindness of physical nature, and is translated to the other world, designated in the case of Lazarus as 'Abraham's bosom' (Luke 16:22) and, in the case of the thief on the cross who believed, as 'paradise' " (Luke 23:43).[1] In other words, having passed "from vice to virtue" and from the outward life to the inward one, there is one last passage to be accomplished, a last Passover, and that is to pass out of the body and out of the world. A last Red Sea to be crossed: that of death. A prayer usually recited at the bedside of the dying reminds us of this meaning of death as being a passover or an exodus: "Go forth from this world, O Christian soul. . . ."

1. *From waiting for the Parousia to the doctrine of the Four Last Things*

Let us see how death, our death, fits into a treatment of the paschal mystery. In the Christian Passover from the outset there was a strong eschatological component which took the form of an intense expectation of Christ's second coming. To the traditional question, "Why do we keep watch tonight?", an author at the beginning of the third century replied: "The reason is twofold: because in it Christ received life after he had suffered, and in it he will later receive the kingdom of the world."[2] The notion of the parousia was so much alive in the Easter vigil that, according to St. Jerome, the bishop had no right to send the people home before midnight, since until that hour it was always possible that the Bridegroom might come, that the parousia might take place.[3]

Furthermore, it was believed that the last night of the world, like its first, would occur at Eastertide.

The point, however, must be made that expectation of the parousia was never the principal content of the Christian Passover (despite what some people have maintained), any more than it was ever the commemoration of creation, which is also present in the liturgy of the feast. At Easter, Christians gathered above all to commemorate the death and resurrection of Christ, the completion of the work of salvation, and not to await or anticipate his return. The main content of the feast has always been historical and commemorative, even though the atmosphere in which it took place might be eschatological.

With the passing of time, an evolution can be observed. From eschatology there is a transition to *anagogy*. In a certain sense, the movement is reversed: the idea of the Lord's coming to us is gradually replaced by that of our going to him, his return to earth by our going to heaven. Likewise general eschatology or eschatology "of the Church" gives way to individual eschatology or eschatology "of the soul." The preoccupation with *when* the Lord's return will occur gradually fades away, leaving instead the basic conviction *that* the Lord will return. And this keeps alive that sense of urgency and immediacy, and consequently of vigilance, characteristic of Christians; henceforth it is not the expectation of the parousia, but of those things which in later times would be known as the *Novissimi*, the Four Last Things. The Easter vigil itself became symbolic of eternal life: "By keeping vigil," says St. Augustine, "we commemorate that night in which the Lord rose and for us inaugurated that eternal life where there is neither death nor sleep."[4]

This was not some makeshift solution but the product of increased maturity of faith. It has been rightly written that this whole process of transformation of eschatology was not prompted by disappointment over the delay of the parousia, but rather by enthusiasm for its fulfillment. "The *eschaton* which was to have come was transformed into an eternal presence, experienced in worship and in spirit. Not deceived hopes but rather the presumed fulfillment of all hopes lay at the root of this transformation" (J. Moltmann).

As always, the Tradition of the Church was the ambiance in which this development occurred and the place where its memory has been preserved. Tradition has collected everything in Scripture which refers to the final fulfillment of salvation into a particular sense called anagogy, as a third aspect or level of spiritual interpretation, after the typological and moral ones. The doctrine of the four senses of Scripture was summed up in the middle ages in the famous couplet:

> The *letter* tells what has happened,
> the *allegory* what you should believe,
> The *moral* what you should do,
> the *anagogy* what you should aspire to.[5]

Applying this schema to the Passover, a medieval author says perfectly consistently: "Easter can have an historical, an allegorical, a moral, and an anagogic sense. Historically, the Passover occurred when the exterminating angel passed through Egypt; allegorically, when, in baptism, the Church passes from infidelity to faith; morally, when the soul, by means of confession and contrition, passes from vice to virtue; anagogically, when we pass from the misery of this life to the eternal joys."[6]

Eschatology thus survives in Christian awareness and in the Easter liturgy in the form of a constant orientation towards things above (cf. Col 3:1), towards the eternal Easter, as a constant reminder of our latter end and true goal. For, translated literally, *anagogia* means "lifting up."

I have begun with these brief observations so as to show from what direction and by what title the first of the Four Last Things, (death) comes into a treatment of the paschal mystery, for that is precisely what we shall be considering next. We shall subsequently see too that this is not the only title by which death forms part of the paschal mystery: there is another, deeper, more essential one.

2. *Death considered sapientially*

One can look at death either in a sapiential way, which the Bible shares with other realities such as philosophy, other religions, poetry; or in a mysterial or paschal way, which is peculiar and exclusive to Christianity. In the former death is pedagogic; in the latter, it is mystagogic, in the sense that it conducts us into the mystery and is itself part of the Christian mystery. As grace supposes nature and transcends it without denying it, so the mysterial or paschal view of death illuminates and goes beyond the natural one, though without making it valueless. The two views stand in relation to one another as the Old and New Testaments. The Old Testament offers us a sapiential vision of death, the New Testament a vision that is mysterial, Christological, and paschal.

So let us begin by considering death in the sapiential perspective. I said the Old Testament offers us an essentially sapiential vision of death; and in point of fact the sapiential books are the only ones that speak about death directly. Job, the Psalms, Ecclesiastes, Sirach, Wisdom: all these books pay considerable attention to the subject of death. "Teach us to number our days aright," says one of the psalms, "that we may gain wisdom of heart" (Ps 90:12). Only in the Book of Wisdom, which is one of the latest of the sapiential books, does the concept of otherworldly reward begin to make death a trace less gloomy.

I have mentioned already that the answers of biblical wisdom on this topic are not essentially different from those put forward by other, profane wisdoms. For Epicurus, death is a begging of the question: "When I am," he used to say, "death is not; when death is, I am not." Therefore it doesn't concern us. There is no point in thinking about it. When a man is born, St. Augustine said, people make all sorts of conjectures: perhaps he will be handsome, perhaps he will be ugly; perhaps he will be rich, perhaps he will be poor; perhaps he will have a long life, perhaps not. . . . But we never say of anyone: perhaps he will die, or perhaps he will not die. This is the one thing about life that is absolutely certain. When we hear that someone is sick with dropsy (the incurable disease of those days; today there are other ones), we say: "Poor wretch, he's going to die; he's doomed, there's nothing for it." But shouldn't we say the same thing when someone is born? "Poor wretch, he's going to die, there's nothing for it, he's doomed!" What difference does it make if it comes a little later or a little sooner? Death is the fatal illness we catch by being born.[7] Perhaps, rather than a mortal life, ours ought to be thought of as a "vital death," a living while dying.[8]

This last thought has been taken up in a secularized key by Heidegger, who very rightly makes death a part of the substance of philosophy. Defining life and the human being as "a being-towards-death,"[9] he treats death not as an incident putting an end to life but as the very substance of life, what life is made of. Living is dying. Human beings cannot live without burning up and shortening their lives, without dying all the time. Living-towards-death means that death is not only the end, but also the purpose of life. We are born in order to die, not for any other purpose. This is a most radical inversion of the Christian view, according to which we are beings-towards-eternity.

More recently, a new wisdom, unknown to the ancients, has been taking an interest in death: psychology. There are psychologists who see the "no to death" as the true meaning of all human activity, of which the sex instinct, held by Freud to be the basis of everything, would only be one manifestation.[10]

But maybe the poets are still the ones to say the simplest and truest sapiential words about death. One of them describes the situation and state of mind of an individual confronting the mystery of death and its silent inevitability like this:

> We are
> like the leaves
> on the trees
> in autumn (G. Ungaretti).

The characteristic of all this human wisdom concerning death is that it does not console, does not dissolve fear. It is like the winter sun, lighting but giving no warmth nor thawing the frost. Every culture and epoch, faced with death as an insoluble riddle, has tried to unravel it, construing it this way and that, formulating it out loud in the hope of finding a key to the enigma. But this enigma is a special one: it does not wait to be solved. Before we can unravel it, it unravels us and sweeps us away. Rather like someone trying to study the movement of waves in the sea, while balancing on a plank just above them: before he can get down to work, a wave has already flung him onto the beach.

3. *Death in its paschal context*

In the New Testament too we find sapiential sayings about death, broadly reminiscent of those in the Old Testament. God's exclamation to the rich man: "You fool, this night your life will be demanded of you; and the things you have prepared, to whom will they belong?" (Luke 12:20) is a reworking of Ecclesiastes and Sirach (cf. Sir 11:19; Eccl 2:21). But there is nothing new in this. If Jesus had confined himself to saying this sort of thing, the human situation vis-à-vis death would not have altered much. It is when he dies for us on the cross, when "one dies for all," that things alter radically and death itself becomes something new. Jesus had spoken of his death as of a paschal exodus (cf. Luke 9:31) and St. John orientates his whole Gospel in such a way as to make it absolutely clear that Christ's death on the cross is the new Passover. Indeed the evangelist invents a new meaning for the word *Passover*, so that he can make it mean Christ's death: the Passover is "the passing of Christ from this world to the Father" (cf. John 13:1). Passover and Christ's death are henceforth so intimately united as to give Christians who knew no philology the notion that the very term *Pascha* was derived from *passio* (passion) and was called this because of Christ's death.

Not only, however, is it death's name that is changed; its nature changes too. Human beings are born to die, says the philosopher. This phrase which, taken literally, as we have seen, is the very antithesis of the Christian view, when read with believing eyes now seems instead to be the perfect formulation of the Christian mystery itself. For of Christ it has been said that he "was born so that he could die."[11]

He, God, took a mortal body so that, in it, he could struggle with and overcome death. Death, the Fathers said, attacked Christ, devoured him (as it was used to doing to all human beings) but was not able "to digest him" since God was in him; thus death was slain by him. "Thanks to the Spirit who could not die, Christ put death to death, who slew the human race."[12] The liturgy, Eastern and Latin alike, has synthesized this dramatic vision of the redemption in a line which it never tires of repeating during Eastertide: "Dying, he has destroyed death."

Human death is no longer what it was. A decisive fact has intervened. In faith we grasp the unbelievable novelty that only the coming to earth of a God could bring about. Death has lost its sting, like a snake whose poison from now on can only send its victim to sleep for an hour or two but cannot kill. "Death is swallowed up in victory. / Where, O death, is your victory? / Where, O death, is your sting?" (1 Cor 15:55).

The last wall has been broken down. Between us and God three walls of separation used to rise: nature, sin, and death. The wall of nature was broken down at the incarnation, when human nature and divine nature were united in the person of Christ; the wall of sin was broken down on the cross, and the wall of death at the resurrection. Death is no more a wall against which all is shattered, but has become a door, a passage, that is to say, literally a Passover. It is a Red Sea thanks to which we enter the Promised Land.

For Jesus did not die just for himself; he did not merely leave us an example of a heroic death, like Socrates. He did something quite different. "One died for all, therefore all have died" (2 Cor 5:14). Jesus "tasted death for everyone" (Heb 2:9). An extraordinary statement which only fails to make us shout for joy because we do not take it as seriously and as literally as it deserves. I repeat: God is involved! Jesus can do this because he is also God. And he alone can do it. Baptized into Christ's death (cf. Rom 6:3), we have entered into a real, even though mystical, relationship with that death, we have become participants in it, such that the Apostle is bold enough, in faith, to proclaim: "You have died" (Col 3:3). Since henceforth we belong to Christ much more than to ourselves (cf. 1 Cor 6:19-20), it follows that, conversely, what is Christ's belongs to us much more than what is ours. His death is more ours than our own death. St. Paul is possibly alluding to this meaning when he tells Christians: "The world, life, *death*, the present, the future: all belong to you because you belong to Christ" (cf. 1 Cor 3:22-23). Death belongs to us more than we belong to it!

So our own death too, and not only Christ's, has become a Passover. St. Ambrose wrote a short work called *Death as a Good (De bono mortis)* and the title itself signifies the change that has taken place. In this work, he says, among other things: "Death is a passage for all, but you must pass with constancy—a passage from corruption to incorruption, from mortality to immortality, from disquiet to tranquillity. And so, do not let the word 'death' alarm you, but let the benefits of a good passage fill you with joy."[13] He applies to death, as we see, the same definition as elsewhere he gives to the Passover. As much as to say: it is called death but it is a Passover!

Our own death does not, therefore, enter into the sphere of the paschal mystery only as one of the Four Last Things, but also for a deeper, more essential reason. Not only on account of what there is ahead of it, but also on account of what there is behind it. Not only on account of the way of eschatology, but also on account of the way of history. No longer is it just a terrifying tutor teaching us how to live, a threat and a deterrent; death has become a mystagogue, a way of penetrating to the heart of the Christian mystery. In dying, the Christian can say in all truth: "Yet I die, no longer I, but Christ dies in me."

4. *Face to face with death for the Christian*

Let us now leave the theory and pass on to consider the practical effects. How have Christians lived that novelty brought by Christ, his victory over death? I cannot now, nor could I, make an exhaustive survey of this. One thing however I can do (and this is more telling): reflect on how I myself have learned about death, how it has been transmitted to me by the Christian environment in which I was born and grew up, and invite my readers to do the same.

We all have indelible memories of what used to constitute the ritualization of death, at home and in church: singing, ceremonies, customs. Death was endued with its own solemnity. There was certainly nothing commonplace about it. Later, however, I came to see there was something missing in this attitude to death, from the truly Christian point of view. It was in great part the religious legacy of the seventeenth and eighteenth centuries, a period that gave the Church a vast number of saints and certainly should not be discounted, but which had lost, at many points, living contact with the word of God and become somewhat impoverished thereby. The dominant attitude to death was not mysterial but sapiential. Death was seen essentially as a teacher of how to live, a deterrent to vice, a severe tutor. The taste for the macabre, although not new in art, now overflowed into forms far from artistic: crypts decorated with human bones and open to the public, skulls everywhere. All pictures of saints painted during this period contain a skull, even pictures of St. Francis of Assisi who had called death "Sister Death." This is a sort of criterion for dating a picture. Above all, the macabre held sway in books of meditations on death.

Almost all of us have personally witnessed the collapse and rapid disappearance of this sort of religiosity of death. A nonbelieving culture, whether Marxist or otherwise, has levelled many a shaft against it. "Christians think about death and not about life. They are more concerned with the other world than with this one and its needs. They are disloyal to Earth. They waste on

Heaven the treasures that rightly belong to Earth." Or: "The Church uses the fear of death as a way of controlling people's minds."

Thus, little by little, what has happened to the idea of eternity has also happened to the idea of death: banished from the Christian pulpit. A flag hauled down. This is a well-attested fact: no one now mentions the Four Last Things. There is a kind of dishonesty and embarrassment in dealing with them. Secular and lay culture, for its part, has chosen the way of repressing the thought of death. Death has become taboo. Nice people do not talk about it in public. Having no useful answer to offer on the subject, modern society has chosen silence; in fact, a conspiracy of silence.

As always, the breakdown of the Christian value has a twofold cause: the external assault of secular culture, and the internal clouding over of the way in which we live and proclaim the value in question. The resumption and renewal of authentic Christian preaching on the Four Last Things and in particular on death cannot consist, obviously, in a return to the forms of another age, to the spirituality inherited from the seventeenth and eighteenth centuries. We need to salvage all that was good and efficacious in it, but to put it into a new context corresponding to the thought patterns of the Church today.

A note in the Vatican II Constitution on the Sacred Liturgy, brief but of great import, laid down: "The rite for the burial of the dead should evidence more clearly the paschal character of Christian death."[14] This being so, we must do all we can to recover that vision of death which I have called mysterial and paschal. The introduction to the new *Order of the Burial of the Dead* begins as follows: "The Christian funeral liturgy is a celebration of the paschal mystery of Christ the Lord." In the prefaces and prayers for the dead, every effort is made to translate this spirit into practice. In the Constitution on the Church in the Modern World (*Gaudium et spes*), the council devoted particular attention to the problem of death and tried to provide answers rooted in the Christian paschal mystery to the worrying questions which human beings are always asking themselves about death.

These directives, in some cases, have already borne marvelous fruit. In environments and communities where the faith is lived, to experience funerals that are little by little being transformed into authentic paschal liturgies—with all the distinctive signs, e.g., the singing of the Alleluia, serenity, festive spirit—is now by no

117

means uncommon. Taking part in them, one seems to see St. Paul's words come true: Death has been transformed into victory (cf. 1 Cor 15:55). This can occur even when the tragic deaths of young people are involved; in such cases, formidable Christian testimony is given, a true epiphany of faith occurs.

5. *"Do you believe?"*

Even so, we cannot sit back satisfied. What I have mentioned are still the exceptions. Today we lack those actions, signs, and words which in days gone by conveyed a total vision and impressed it indelibly on the mind. Perhaps this is no longer even possible. When I was a boy, those words were virtually the only ones that stood out against the words of everyday, the only ones heard and sung with other people. People arrived in church from work with "virgin ears." Nowadays, we are beset with words, music, and images. Nothing said can hold its place long in the mind before something new chases it out. It is a new culture, and we have to proclaim the gospel in it nevertheless, without waiting for the culture to change. What are the means at our disposal? Once again: proclamation, the ministry of the word. For the word of God has not ceased being "like fire, like a hammer shattering rocks" (Jer 23:29). It has not stopped being different from human words and being stronger than they are.

What are we to proclaim to one another and to other people? "Dying you destroyed our death . . .," we say in the Mass immediately after the consecration. When we are considering death, the most important thing in Christianity is not the fact that we have to die, but the fact that Christ has died. Christianity has no need of the fear of death to make its way. It makes its way by Christ's death. Jesus came to free the human race from the fear of death, not to increase it. The Son of God, we read in the Letter to the Hebrews, took flesh and blood like us so "that, through death, he might destroy the one who has the power of death, that is, the devil, and free those who through fear of death had been subject to slavery all their life" (Heb 2:14-15). It is a terrible error, a reprehensible distortion, that people should have come to believe the opposite. We can never preach too much about this.

We ought also to create a store of religious certainties within us, elementary as they may be, yet so rooted in our very marrow that we can pass them on to other people, not as matters of doctrine but as facts of life. If Jesus has died for all, if he "tasted death on behalf of all," this means that death is no longer that unknown, that "undiscovered country from whose bourn no traveller returns."[15] People say: You're on your own, when the moment comes we all die alone; no one can die in my place; each of us, once and all alone, has to cross this fearsome "bridge of sighs"; it's stupid to talk about dying as though it were an impersonal event, since I'm the one who does the dying and no one can do it with me or for me.

But this is no longer true, since someone has died instead of me. Here we have to take the offensive, here we have to entrench ourselves in the faith, without retreating in the face of any attack by skepticism, whether it comes from within us or outside us. "If we have died with him, we shall also live with him" (2 Tim 2:11). If we have died "with him" . . . So it *is* possible to die as a twosome!

It is the same problem as Jesus put to Martha: Do you believe, yes or no? Ah, if only you had been here! says Martha, and Jesus replies: "I am the Resurrection and the Life; whoever believes in me, even if he dies, will live . . . Do you believe this?" (John 11:21-26). Being a Christian means precisely that: not other cultural or political notions or anything else. It means being united to Christ for life and for death, being a member of a head who has passed through death for each member.

What makes the fact of death so unlike anything else is that we do not know what it is until we have experienced it and those who have experienced it are no longer in a position to talk about it. For it is impossible to anticipate one's own death, to domesticate it, to take it a little at a time, so as to see what it is like, as one can everything else. It is beyond our grasp. We cannot neutralize it by taking it in small doses, like the famous poison of Mithridates. We have to tackle it all at once, *semel*, as the Letter to the Hebrews says (Heb 9:27). We die only once.

The terrible seriousness of death! Yet in Christ even this aspect is different. He has tasted death on my behalf, my death. He has gone before me. To the degree to which I identify myself with him, grow into him, I take control of my own death, in a certain sense I experience it. With St. Paul, I can say, "Every day I face death; *quotidie morior*" (1 Cor 15:31).

That same Apostle wrote these illuminating words: "None of us lives for oneself, and no one dies for oneself. For if we live, we live for the Lord, and if we die, we die for the Lord; so then, whether we live or die, we are the Lord's" (Rom 14:7-8). What does he mean? That, since Christ, the greatest antithesis is no longer between living and dying, but between living for oneself and living for the Lord. If one lives for the Lord, death and life seem merely two different ways of being with him: first in danger, then in safety.

Henceforth there is an efficacious remedy against the fear of death. From time immemorial, people have never stopped looking for remedies against death. One of these remedies is called "progeny": survival in one's children. Yet another remedy, bound up with Marxist ideology, is called "the race" or "the species": we cease as individual and person but survive in the human race, which is immortal. In our own day, there is widespread belief in a new remedy: reincarnation. But this is silly. People who profess this doctrine as an integral part of their culture and religion are well aware that it is no remedy or consolation, but a punishment. The soul is reincarnated because it still has something more to expiate; and if it is to expiate, it has to suffer. Reincarnation can serve any purpose except that of providing consolation in face of death. There is only one true remedy for death: Jesus Christ; and woe betide us Christians if we do not proclaim this to the world.

6. *What death can teach us*

Should we perhaps conclude that the sapiential consideration of death is useless henceforward; that, having known death as a mystagogue, we no longer need death as a tutor? No! Christ's paschal victory over death forms part of the *kerygma*. But we know that the *kerygma* does not annul, but is rather the basis of, *paraenesis*, the summons to conversion of manners.

Since Christ, the sapiential consideration of death retains the same function that the law had before the coming of grace. It too serves to guard love and grace. The law, it is written, was given for sinners (cf. 1 Tim 1:9), and we are still sinners, subject to the seduction of the world and things visible, always tempted to "conform ourselves to the world." "When it is morning," *The*

Imitation of Christ exhorts us, "think you will not live till evening. And when evening comes, venture not to promise yourself the next morning."[16] This was why the Desert Fathers so cultivated the thought of death as to make it their constant practice, a kind of cornerstone of their spirituality, and to keep it alive by every means. One of them, who worked by spinning wool, adopted the habit of every now and then symbolically letting the spindle drop to the ground and "putting death before his eyes before he picked it up again."[17] They were in love with the idea of sobriety, and the thought of death is the one most apt to create the state of sobriety in human beings. It destroys illusions, vain raptures, and empty ecstasies. It leads into most absolute truth.

Looking at life from the observation post of death is extraordinarily helpful for leading a good life. Are you vexed by problems and difficulties? Hurry yourself forward, adopt the right position: look at these things from your deathbed. How then would you wish to have acted? What importance would you attach to these matters? Act like this and you will be safe! You have a quarrel with someone? Look at it from your deathbed. What would you wish you had done then: won, or been shamed? Come off best, or forgiven?

Death-the-tutor guards grace and is at the service of death-the-mystery in another way too. For it prevents us from becoming attached to things and fixing the heart's dwelling here below, forgetting that "here below we have no continuing city" (cf. Heb 13:14). When we die, says one of the psalms, "we shall take nothing with us; our wealth will not follow us down" into the grave (cf. Ps 49:18).

Death-the-tutor is also useful to us because it teaches us to be vigilant, to be prepared. In death, the strangest combination of opposites occurs: certainty and uncertainty. Of all things it is at once the most certain and least certain: most certain *that* it will be, least certain *when* it will be. "Therefore, stay awake, for you know neither the day nor the hour" (Matt 25:13). Any moment may be the appointed time. One day David, being pursued by Saul, made this exclamation, which has always impressed me with its universal truth: "As the LORD lives, . . . there is but a step between me and death!" (1 Sam 20:3). It is always true, even now, for all of us: we are but one step away from death. Death is round the corner! How many people are taking that "step" at this very moment! It is estimated that thousands of people die every minute and many of them have not given much more thought to death than we have just been giving.

Sister Death is certainly a good elder sister. She can teach us much, if only we are willing to listen to her docilely. The Church is not afraid to put us to school to her. In the Ash Wednesday liturgy there is a powerfully worded antiphon (it sounds even more powerful in the original Latin, especially if sung to the Gregorian chant): "Direct our hearts to better things, O Lord; heal our sin and ignorance. Lord, do not face us suddenly with death but give us time to repent." A Lent, a day, a single hour, a good confession: how differently we should look on such things in that moment! How much we should prefer them to sceptres and kingdoms, long life, wealth and health!

Death-the-mystagogue does not chase Death-the-pedagogue away but seeks her out and honors her, just as grace does not chase the law away but seeks it out and willingly submits to it, knowing that the law defends us from our worst enemy, our inconstancy and thoughtlessness. Death-the-pedagogue has even made saints. There was, in the Middle Ages, a brilliant young man full of high hopes who, looking one day at the corpse of a dead relative, heard a voice issue from it: "What you are, so once was I; what I am, so shall you be." The thought gave him such a shock that of the worldly youth it made a saint: St. Sylvester Gozzolini, abbot.

7. *Death, the Christian preacher*

Another environment besides the spiritual and ascetic comes to mind in which we have a pressing need for Sister Death as teacher: evangelization. The thought of death is just about the only weapon left us for jolting an affluent society out of its torpor. What has happened to the West happened to the chosen people after being liberated from Egypt: "Jacob ate his fill, the darling grew fat and frisky; you became fat and gross and gorged; you forgot the God who had made you" (cf. Deut 32:15). When in a society the citizens lose all sense of restraint and allow no obstacle to hold them back from doing what they want, when there is no other way of saving them from chaos, what is to be done? The death penalty is enacted. I am not saying this is right; I only mean that, in another sense, we too ought to re-introduce the "death penalty." We should remind people again of this ancient punishment, which has never been repealed: "You are dust, and to dust you shall return" (Gen 3:19). "Memento mori": remember you have to die!

At a critical moment in the chosen people's history, God said to the prophet Isaiah: "Cry out!" The prophet replied: "What shall I cry out?" God said: "All mankind is grass, / and all their glory like the flower of the field. / The grass withers, the flower wilts, / when the breath of the LORD blows upon it. . . . / The grass withers, the flower wilts" (Isa 40:6-7). I think God is giving the same order today to his prophets, and he is doing this because he loves his children and does not want them "to be herded like sheep into the nether world, death being their shepherd" (cf. Ps 49:15).

Death is herself a great Christian preacher. She truly preaches "timely and untimely" (cf. 2 Tim 4:2). She preaches from every nook and cranny: indoors, out of doors, in the country and in the town, from the newspapers and television. She does it even through the leaves on the trees in autumn as we have been told. No one can silence her. We have no choice but to hear her. What a formidable ally we have in her, if only we take the trouble to back her up, lend her voice, and gather an audience for her!

But how—one will say—are we to revive the fear of death? Didn't Jesus come to set free those who were held prisoner by the fear of death? Yes, but we have to have known this fear before we can be set free from it. Jesus frees those from the fear of death who have it, not those who do not have it, who blithely ignore the fact that they will have to die. He came to put fear into those who don't have it and to take it away from those who do have it. He came to teach fear of eternal death to those who only knew fear of temporal death. If people will not let themselves be persuaded to do what is right for love of eternal life, let they at least be dissuaded from doing what is wrong for fear of eternal death.

The "second death," the Book of Revelation calls it (Rev 20:6). What is the "second death?" It is the only one that really deserves to be called death, since it is not a passing, not a Passover, but an end, a terrible terminus. Nor is it pure and simple nothingness. No, it is a despairing rush towards nothingness in order to escape from God and oneself, without, however, ever being able to achieve it. It is an eternal death, in the sense of an eternal dying, a chronic death. But this is to say nothing about what it is really like. Our having a feeble idea of sin, someone has observed, pertains to our sinful nature. I for my part say that our having a feeble idea of eternity pertains to our temporal nature. Our having a feeble idea of death pertains to our still being alive.

It is to save our brothers and sisters from this disaster that we ought to start preaching about death again. Who better than St. Francis of Assisi knew the new, paschal face of Christian death? His death was a truly paschal passing, a *transitus*, and it is by this name that it is commemorated by his spiritual children on the vigil of his feast. When he felt his end was near, the Poverello "asked that the Gospel according to St. John be read to him from the place that begins: 'Before the feast of the Passover . . .' (John 13:1) and at the end he exclaimed, "Welcome, my Sister Death!"[18] Yet, in his *Canticle of the Creatures,* alongside very loving words about death, he also has some of the most terrible: "Woe to those who die in mortal sin! Happy those she finds doing your will! The second death can do no harm to them."

"The sting of death is sin," says the Apostle (1 Cor 15:56). Sin is what gives death its fearsome power to distress and strike fear into people. For people who live in mortal sin, death still retains its sting, its poison, as before the coming of Christ, and for this reason it can wound, kill, and send to Gehenna. Do not be afraid, Christ said, of the death which kills the body and after that can do no more. Be afraid of that death which, having killed the body, has the power to cast into Gehenna (cf. Luke 12:4-5). Having taken sin away, you have taken death's sting away too!

8. *Born so that we can die*

In instituting the Eucharist, Jesus anticipated his own death. He did as the prophets of old had done, who by their symbolic actions—such as the smashing of a pitcher—not only foretold what was going to happen but anticipated it, grafting the future into history. So Jesus, in breaking the bread and distributing the cup, anticipated his own death, gave it the meaning he intended it to have and lived it in private with his disciples before being overwhelmed by the external event and the howling crowd of enemies, who put a very different construction on that death.

We can do the same, for Jesus invented this way to make us sharers in his death, so as to unite us to him. Taking part in the Eucharist is the truest, rightest, most effective way of preparing ourselves for death. In it we celebrate our own death as well as Christ's and offer it, day by day, to the Father, for Christ "has died for all and hence all have died." In the Eucharist, we can raise our own "Amen, yes," to the Father, to what he expects of us, to the kind of death he intends to allow for us, for we can make Jesus himself our "Amen to God" (cf. 2 Cor 1:20). In the Eucharist, we ourselves bear witness: we decide to whom we shall bequeath our life and for whom we shall die.

I said already that the definition of human beings as "beings-towards-death" applies perfectly to Christ, who was born "so that he could die." But it applies to Christians too. Why be born, if we have to die? the skeptic asks. Who has "thrown and hurled" us into this our existence? the existentialist philosopher wonders. By faith, we know the answer. We are born so that we can die. But this does not seem to be a death sentence; actually, we look on it as a privilege. We have received the gift of life, so as to have something unique, precious, worthy of God, for us in our turn to be able to offer him as gift and sacrifice. What worthier use can one imagine for life than to make a gift of it, for love, to the creator who loves us? We can adapt for ourselves the words the priest utters at the offertory of the Mass over the bread and wine, and say, "Through your goodness we have received this gift of life to offer; may it become a holy and living sacrifice pleasing to you" (cf. Rom 12:1).

For this, however, we need the Holy Spirit. It is written that Christ offered himself to God "through the eternal Spirit" (cf. Heb 9:14). The Holy Spirit it was who raised the impulse of self-giving in the Redeemer's soul, leading him to accept his own death as a sacrifice.

So, have we rid our life of all natural fear and anguish about death? No, but that is not what matters. The victory does not happen in nature, but in faith, and it is possible therefore that nature itself derives no benefit. Jesus himself was willing to experience "a sorrow even to death" in his soul at the thought of imminent death, and explained this by saying, "The spirit is willing, but the flesh is weak" (Matt 26:41). Even of this anguish we can make material to be offered in the Eucharist, with Jesus, to the Father. Christ has redeemed our fear as well!

What really counts is faith. To every disciple, the Risen Jesus repeats what he once said to Martha: "I am the resurrection and the life; whoever believes in me, even if he dies, will live; and everyone who lives and believes in me will never die. Do you believe this? Blessed are those who feel able to reply, by God's grace, from the depths of the heart: "Yes, Lord, I believe!"

NOTES

1. Origen, *In Numeros* 26.4 (GCS 30, p. 249).
2. Lactantius, *Divinarum institutionum* 7.19.3 (CSEL 19, p. 645).
3. Cf. St. Jerome, *In Matthaeum* 4.25.6 (CCL 77, p. 236f.).
4. St. Augustine, *Sermo* 221.4 (*Miscellanea Agostiniana* 1, p. 460).
5. "Littera gesta docet, quid credas allegoria.
   Moralis quid agas, quo tendas anagogia."
6. Sicardus of Cremona, *Mitrale* 6.15 (PL 213, 543).
7. St. Augustine, *Sermo* 229, *Sermo Guelferbytanus* 12.3 (*Misc. Agost.* 1, p. 482f.).
8. St. Augustine, *Confessions* 1.6.7.
9. M. Heidegger, *Being and Time* 2.1.51.
10. Cf. E. Becker, *The Denial of Death,* The Free Press 1973.
11. St. Gregory of Nyssa, *Oratio catechetica* 32 (PG 45, 80); St. Augustine, *Sermo* 23A.3 (CCL 41, p. 322).
12. Melito of Sardis, *On Pascha* 66 (SCh 123, p. 96).
13. St. Ambrose, *De bono mortis* 4.15 (CSEL 32, 1, p. 716f.).
14. *Sacrosanctum Concilium* 81.
15. W. Shakespeare, *Hamlet,* III, sc. 1.
16. *Imitation of Christ* 1.23.
17. *Apophthegms of the Coislin MS* 126 n. 58.
18. Celano, *Vita secunda* 163, 217 (*Writings,* cit., p. 536).

Also by *Raniero Cantalamessa*

Easter in the Early Church
An Anthology of Jewish and Early Christian Texts

This anthology of texts for students and preachers presents the authentic Christian traditions about Easter.
2164-3   Paper, 268 pp., 5 3/8 x 8 1/4, $19.95
Rights: World

Mary, Mirror of the Church

While this work cannot help but discuss aspects of Mariology, it is not so much a study as it is a pilgrimage. Reflecting on and following Mary's example, as Father Cantalamessa presents it here, we enter into a pilgrimage of listening and obedience to God's Word.
2059-0   Paper, 224 pp., 5 3/8 x 8 1/4, $11.95
Rights: World

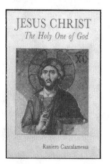

Jesus Christ, the Holy One of God

In his meditations Father Cantalamessa has approached the person of Christ by following the classic statements of the Church: Jesus Christ is true man, he is true God, he is one sole person. Of the six reflections two are devoted to the humanity of Christ, two to his divinity, and two to his unity of person. The concluding chapter is a kind of excursus, which amounts to a critical evaluation of the theses recently advanced in certain so-called "new Christologies," more particularly on the problem of the divinity of Christ.
2073-6   Paper, 172 pp., 5 3/8 x 8 1/4, $6.95
Rights: U.S. and Canada

Available from

THE LITURGICAL PRESS
P.O. Box 7500, Collegeville, MN 56321
Phone: 1-800-858-5450; Fax: 1-800-445-5899

Prices subject to change without notice.